Contents

About the Downloadable Materials

Purchasers of this book may download, print, and/or photocopy these forms found in the Appendix for educational use: Behavior Progress Report (Primary Classroom), Behavior Progress Report (Intermediate/Middle Level Classroom), and Behavior Progress Report (Multiple Secondary Classrooms). These materials are included with the print book and are also available at **www.brookespublishing.com/knoster/materials** for both print and e-book buyers.

About the Authors

Tim Knoster, Ed.D., is a professor at the McDowell Institute for Teacher Excellence in Positive Behavior Support in the College of Education at Bloomsburg University of Pennsylvania. The McDowell Institute emphasizes the translation of research on multi-tiered systems of support—most specifically, positive behavior interventions and supports—into practice in schools. Dr. Knoster has also served as Executive Director of the International Association for Positive Behavior Support since its inception in 2003. Dr. Knoster (or Tim, as he prefers) has been involved with  preservice and in-service teacher training for more than 30 years. He has worn many hats throughout his career, including the role of an instructor of undergraduate and graduate courses, a classroom teacher in the public schools, Director of Student Support Services and Special Education, and Principal Investigator as well as Program Evaluator on federal projects focused on classroom and student-centered behavior intervention and support. Specifically relevant to this book, Dr. Knoster has extensive experience in providing professional development for classroom teachers and has been the recipient of numerous awards for his endeavors in this regard. He has extensively published and provided training for educators and staff from various child-serving systems in the application of positive behavior support in schools and community-based settings. Dr. Knoster has an uncanny ability to help teachers interpret the research literature on behavioral matters in a way that enables them to translate that same research into practical strategies and approaches in their classrooms.

Robin Drogan, Ph.D., is an assistant professor and graduate program coordinator in the Department of Exceptionality Programs at Bloomsburg University of Pennsylvania. She has been involved in the education of individuals with disabilities for more than 20 years. During this time, her roles have included teacher, teacher collaborator, educational and behavioral interventionist, researcher, and author. Her research and practical interests focus on tiered behavioral and academic supports for students, preventive intervention strategies for young children, team collaboration emphasizing teacher involvement, family engagement, and peer support systems within the context of addressing the needs of all students and staff in inclusive settings. Dr. Drogan spends much of her time supporting preservice students in extensive field experiences focusing on the implementation of evidence-based practices and prevention-based strategies.

Preface

Meeting the needs of all students in the classroom is both a noble and challenging pursuit, one that requires the efforts of dedicated teachers working to implement effective educational practices that support every child. Energy, time, and commitment are especially required when it comes to supporting students with behavioral challenges. This book is a follow-up and companion to *The Teacher's Pocket Guide for Effective Classroom Management* (Knoster, 2008, 2014), a book on universal approaches to positive behavior support. *The Teacher's Pocket Guide for Effective Classroom Management* was written to help teachers build a foundation for supporting positive behavior for all students in the classroom. This new book, *The Teacher's Pocket Guide for Positive Behavior Support: Targeted Classroom Solutions,* is written for those teachers working with kids in need of additional (targeted) behavioral supports that build on general classroom structures.

Some who are reading this book may be teaching in school systems that are at various stages of implementing multi-tiered systems of support (MTSS) in the form of positive behavior interventions and supports (PBIS). Others, however, may be teaching in more traditional school settings. Regardless of where you teach, this book will help you to choose appropriate targeted supports for your students and make sure that your approach to behavioral support is a good contextual fit within your school system. We have written this book in conversational language to provide clarity and practical guidance to classroom teachers, translating the literature on targeted behavioral supports for real-world application to your teaching practices.

Chapter 1 introduces the concept of targeted interventions and supports and illustrates their benefit to particular groups of students struggling with behavior through examples and vignettes. In Chapter 2, you will learn about how targeted behavioral supports are implemented in schools that utilize PBIS as well as in traditional school settings. Chapter 3 teaches you how to organize and collect data for identifying students in need of more targeted support and for monitoring student progress. There is also a focus on matching targeted interventions and supports to student needs. Chapter 4 describes the delivery of targeted supports in PBIS schools by highlighting commonly available Tier 2 (targeted) supports while providing guidance on coordinating instructional practices with services outside of school provider systems (e.g., mental health services). Chapter 5 offers more in-depth guidance in terms of steps for planning and selecting targeted supports for use in classrooms within traditional schools that have not established MTSS in the form of PBIS. Case stories and student profiles are used in both Chapters 4 and 5 to illustrate the practices described in PBIS and traditional school settings. In Chapter 6, we provide guidance on how to adjust targeted supports over time based on student progress as assessed through practical analysis of instructional data. Finally, in Chapter 7, we describe the relationship between targeted supports (Tier 2) and individualized intensive supports (Tier 3) and provide a general overview of developing a multicomponent behavior support plan based on the results of functional behavioral assessment.

We hope that you find this book useful in your daily work with students, particularly those requiring more extensive behavioral interventions and supports. We have created this compact pocket guide in the hope of providing a quick, concise reference that will allow the busy teacher to identify and implement targeted behavioral supports that are consistent, sustainable, and well matched to student needs. Thank you for taking the time to read this book and for your commitment to all kids!

How Are Targeted Supports Different from Universal Supports, and Which Students Will Benefit from Them?

As a teacher, time is likely one of your most precious and fleeting commodities. Thus, we do not want to waste your time in reading (nor did we want to waste our time in writing) this book for its own sake. The most important reason you should read this book is that the content should be helpful if you work directly (or aspire to work directly) with young children or adolescents in a classroom setting. Let's face it—anyone who works with kids in schools knows the rewards and challenges (the proverbial roller coaster ride of emotions with the highs and lows) that are experienced in classrooms on a daily basis. Student behavior is a major cause of or contributing factor to these rewards and challenges. This book—a quick and encouraging guide to behavior interventions for your students who need extra support—can help with some of those challenges.

Teachers have a uniquely personal, firsthand understanding of their students and classrooms through their day-to-day experiences. This understanding enables teachers to organize effective and efficient instructional practices to meet the needs of all their students. However, even if you are an experienced teacher, you will sometimes need ideas for how best to apply your expertise to help certain students or how to reconcile what you know about what works for your students against a context of structures that your school puts into place. As we present strategies and guidance in this book, our goal is to honor and build on your existing frame of reference—both the positive experiences that make you feel good inside, as well as the highly frustrating experiences that, although uncomfortable, have likely helped you to grow as a teacher.

STARTING WITH A FIRM FOUNDATION OF UNIVERSAL APPROACHES

We follow a similar approach to the one used in *The Teacher's Pocket Guide for Effective Classroom Management, Second Edition* (Knoster, 2014). Collectively, the practices highlighted in that book can help teachers to integrate positive behavior support (PBS) at a universal level with all students in the classroom. This foundation of classroom management provides a solid platform upon which to build targeted supports, much like a home's foundation provides a solid base for building. A wide array of universal approaches can help teachers to facilitate the healthy growth and development of their students while also diminishing the likelihood of misbehavior. Table 1.1 provides a brief review of these key universal preventive approaches.

Rather extensive research (see Horner, Sugai, & Anderson, 2010) has been conducted about universal preventive approaches, which can be considered to form the first tier of positive behavior support in the classroom, or Tier 1 in what is often explained as a three-tiered support model. Universal preventive approaches can be summarized simply as preventive classroom management and interpersonal

Table 1.1. Key universal preventive approaches

Universal practice	Brief description of the universal practice
Building rapport (staying close)	The teacher's actions result in each student trusting that the teacher has a genuine interest in him or her as a person. The teacher's behaviors result in a constructive student–teacher relationship that is based on trust and mutual respect.
Establishing/teaching performance expectations	The teacher and the students in the classroom together identify three to five broad expectations (e.g., be responsible, be respectful, be here/be ready) and, in turn, create positively stated operational definitions that reflect what students would look/sound like in meeting the expectations across pivotal contexts in the classroom. Once the expectations are established, direct instruction is provided to the students through simulations, with periodic booster sessions over the course of the school year.
Positive reinforcement (behavior-specific praise)	The teacher's presentation of a desired stimulus (e.g., verbal praise in the instance where the student finds verbal praise rewarding) is contingent on the student(s) acting in a manner that is expected (e.g., the student raising his or her hand to gain the teacher's attention in the classroom). The delivery of the reinforcer (e.g., verbal praise) is explicitly labeled in connection to the behavior that is being reinforced (e.g., "Nice job of raising your hand, Sam. How can I help you?").
Achieving the 4:1 ratio	The teacher, through his or her distribution of positive reinforcement for desired behavior in relation to corrective feedback in response to student problem behavior (misbehavior that requires direct intervention), achieves a ratio of four positive reinforcements for desired behavior to each instance of redirection for problem behavior (thus, the 4:1 ratio). This ratio should ideally be achieved with both the class (in aggregate) and each individual student in the classroom.

relationship strategies; however, it is important to understand that certain approaches need to be applied with fidelity and consistency. Your particular school may be implementing positive behavior interventions and supports (PBIS) on a schoolwide basis (often referred to as schoolwide positive

> Universal approaches are the foundation for positive student behavior across a whole classroom or school.

behavior support, or SWPBS). In such cases, there are likely set expectations, rapport-building structures, and reinforcement systems in place that everyone in the school should employ. Whether or not your school is implementing this framework, it is helpful to know effective universal preventive strategies.

WHAT ARE UNIVERSAL (TIER 1) SUPPORTS, AND WHO ARE THEY FOR?

Universal supports are for everybody. The key components—building rapport, setting clear expectations, and reinforcing desired behavior—are principles that establish a climate conducive to learning. Students will be more engaged in your instruction when it is clear that you care about them (have rapport), when it is clear what they should be doing (set expectations), and when they see that doing what they are supposed to do pays off (reinforcement). Ensuring that these components are addressed in your classroom—whether through your own initiatives or in conjunction with schoolwide procedures—is very much worth the effort. We know from personal teaching experience, as well as research, that using these universal approaches fosters a positive classroom environment and prevents a lot of potential problem behavior.

Establishing Rapport

Most teachers naturally understand that developing rapport with their students is essential for a classroom to function well. When students believe you know them, care about them, and have their best interests at heart, they are more likely to respect the expectations you set and are more receptive to your instruction. However, as would be the case in any human relationship, you will find some students easier to bond with than others. For those students who seem harder to reach, you may need to employ a more systematic approach to develop necessary rapport. Make a conscious effort to be in closer physical proximity, be inviting with your body language and be empathetic with how you talk, find out what the student is interested in and ask open-ended questions about it, and seek out extra occasions to start a conversation with the student. Rapport-building efforts should be comprised of numerous brief interactions. You should expect the process to take some time, or many small interactions, before the student of concern warms up to you (and for you to feel more comfortable with the student).

Setting Clear Expectations

The most effective classrooms are governed by simple, concise, and overarching guiding principles for behavior, not by exhaustive lists of rules. Choosing three to five positively stated, broad behavioral expectations and posting them in your room is encouraged (e.g., "Be responsible, be respectful, and be ready"). In PBIS schools, there are likely already three to five schoolwide expectations like these in place, and you should translate them into your classroom. After identifying these broad expectations, you should identify key settings and routines and operationally define the expectations for those contexts (e.g., "What would my students look and sound like if they are being responsible during group work in my seventh-grade physical science class?"). At the beginning of the school year, instruct the students on the expectations, and provide booster sessions throughout the year.

Reinforcing Positive Behavior

When your students behave appropriately per the classroom expectations, it is important to frequently reinforce that good behavior. Positive reinforcement (i.e., the presentation of a desired stimulus contingent on the performance of a desired behavior in order to increase the likelihood of the future recurrence of that same desired behavior) is great to use in your classroom because it also helps with building and maintaining rapport with your students. Reinforcement can take the form of praise as well as tangible reinforcers and can be delivered in a number of ways, including token economy systems. When determining how often you need to provide reinforcement, you can base the interval on how often you find yourself having to redirect problem behavior. Always aim, at least, for reinforcing appropriate behavior four times for every one instance of redirection or other consequences for problem behavior. Achieving this 4:1 ratio will steer students toward desired behavior and result in a majority of teacher–student interactions being positive.

WHERE THIS BOOK COMES IN: STUDENTS WHO NEED MORE SUPPORT

> Targeted supports are layered on top of universal approaches, offering extra support to a particular group of students.

As valuable as these universal approaches are for teachers, some students will need additional, more targeted support. This book was written to provide guidance to teachers working with students who have not sufficiently responded to universal, or Tier 1, approaches and are in need of additional targeted support.

WILL THIS BOOK HELP ME IN MY CLASSROOM?

We believe you will find this book to be valuable regardless of whether you are an aspiring teacher or a veteran with many years of experience in the classroom. We also firmly believe you will find the targeted strategies and supports emphasized in this book to be useful regardless of the age of your students or other circumstances outside of your control, such as poverty, adverse or traumatic life experiences, or the presence of a disability. The practices and approaches described in this book are based on the literature and reflect evidence-based practice (Brown, Anderson, & De Pry, 2015; Dunlap, Sailor, Horner, & Sugai, 2009; Koegel, Koegel, & Dunlap, 1996). To keep things accessible for you, we wrote this book in a conversational tone, reflecting the plain language we have used in workshops and in-service trainings throughout our teaching careers.

Just as with universal approaches, prevention is the bulls-eye of targeted intervention and supports. Many parts of this book are framed within a preventive context of what has come to be described as a multi-tiered systems of support (MTSS) framework in the form of PBIS. Although more and more schools are implementing PBIS, a large number of school systems have not yet fully adopted such a data-driven approach to organize resources in their local schools. In light of this reality, we provide guidance in this book both for educators who work in schools that have formally adopted a PBIS approach and for educators who are teaching within more traditional school settings. We also provide a list of recommended resources (see Resources) to increase your access to the expansive literature base that supports the practices that we incorporate into these chapters. We are optimistic that you will find this book to be an easy read in terms of concepts and practices.

WHICH STUDENTS CAN THIS BOOK HELP?

All teachers share a common mission to help students learn and grow in a manner that enables each child to develop both academic and social-emotional (behavioral) competence. Some things that affect learning are within your direct influence, such as your pace of instruction, the provision of opportunities to respond, and the reinforcement procedures used with students. However, many students come to school with challenging life experiences that often set the stage for difficulty with learning.

Students Who Have Experienced Trauma

One area of growing concern is student life experiences that reflect varying forms and degrees of trauma. Trauma can be acute or chronic in nature for any particular student. Acute trauma may occur when one of your students experiences a significant event, such as a gang-related violent event in the community, the death of a friend or family member, or a natural disaster (e.g., flood, earthquake). Chronic trauma involves a traumatic event that recurs over time, such as ongoing physical or sexual abuse, neglect, or domestic violence. Traumatic experiences increase the likelihood of the need for intervention and supports that go beyond (but are layered on top of) the universal classroom approaches described previously. The targeted approaches emphasized in this book reflect a trauma-informed approach to working with young children, adolescents, and young adults in schools (Table 1.2). Trauma-informed approaches can help to reverse the demoralizing impact of any past trauma and prevent further traumatization, which in turn can positively alter a student's self-perception, worldview, residual symptoms, and even brain functioning to support learning (Craig, 2008). As a whole, these approaches lead to increases in student motivation, engagement, and participation, thus having a constructive impact on classroom and school climate.

Students Who Do Not Sufficiently Respond to Universal Preventive Approaches

Targeted intervention and supports are appropriate for students who do not sufficiently respond to universal preventive approaches in your classroom. This section presents a view of the process of student learning, as well as how to organize an array of targeted interventions and supports to meet student needs.

With regard to learning and your mission in the classroom, academic, social, emotional, and behavioral growth are all interrelated. It is not uncommon to find that a student who

Table 1.2. Core principles of trauma-informed care in the classroom

Principle	How this principle plays out in the classroom
Safety	Teacher and peer actions within the classroom promote healthy and constructive interactions among people in the classroom, including proper usage of learning materials in tandem with physical items (e.g., furniture, windows, doors). The desired result is that each person in the classroom (students, teachers, visitors) feels safe to take reasonable risks in the learning process free from the fear of possible physical, social, and psychological harm.
Trustworthiness	Teacher and peer actions enable each individual student in the classroom to acquire a sense of confidence and reliance in the integrity and ability of others with whom the student interacts. Honest and clear communication is essential to establishing trust.
Collaboration	Teacher and peer actions demonstrate respect for the contribution of each individual in the classroom in a cooperative learning environment.
Choice	Teacher and peer actions provide opportunities for each student to experience a variety of options for expression of skills within learning activities in the classroom and school in a manner that is sensitive to issues of locus of control.
Strength based	Teacher and peer actions provide opportunities for all students and staff in the classroom to build upon skills that they possess to further extend personal learning.
Culturally, historically, and gender responsive	Teacher and peer actions in tandem with physical attributes of the classroom (and ideally the school) embrace diversity in its many forms and are sensitive to the influence that bias can have on the learning environment.
Empowerment	Teacher and peer actions respect the importance for each individual student and staff member to exercise personal power in decision making to facilitate growth and learning.

is struggling behaviorally is also struggling (or is at greater risk to struggle) academically. Conversely, if history is any indicator, the longer a student struggles academically, the more likely it is that the student may engage in misbehavior (e.g., being disruptive in the classroom to avoid completing

> Students may need targeted supports in just one or multiple areas; the need will vary by individual student and environments.

an undesired task assigned by the teacher). In other words, the students in your classroom are complex, complete human beings—not simply the sum of their parts. It may be necessary to plan and implement both targeted academic and behavioral interventions and supports to effectively meet the needs of students who are chronically struggling to be successful in the classroom.

Now, having noted this reality, we still have some further unpacking to do. The use of the terms *academic* and *behavioral* to describe student learning, although useful, needs to be viewed with a degree of caution. It is important to understand that academic learning and behavioral learning encompass many different forms and variations of student learning.

A LOOK AT STUDENTS WHO MAY BENEFIT FROM TARGETED SUPPORTS

As noted, many possible factors affect and make up student learning, academically and behaviorally; these factors in turn shape the areas and types of intervention a student may need. To illustrate, let's consider some example students, all of whom will be revisited and explored in greater depth in later chapters.

Alexa

Alexa is an eighth-grade student who has been increasingly disruptive in the classroom and cutting class at her middle school. Over time, a pattern has emerged: She appears to mainly act out or cut class during the third instructional block of the day, which is integrated math and science. In these two courses, Alexa struggles in terms of performance on assignments, projects, and examinations. Upon further investigation by the teachers at school, while Alexa is struggling both academically and behaviorally in math and science, she is actually performing sufficiently well in social studies and the performing arts and reasonably well in her English class (with some additional reading support from the teacher). Alexa, although challenged by the course content, is also performing reasonably well in Spanish.

Alexa is an example of a student who has both academic and behavioral concerns. However, it is neither accurate nor particularly helpful to simply say she is struggling academically or behaviorally. It is necessary to be sufficiently precise when looking at Alexa in terms of her academic and behavioral performance. It is also important to avoid labeling Alexa using broad terms, such as being a "good student" or "poor student" or a "universal/Tier 1 student" or "targeted/Tier 2 student." This is not to suggest that labels and terms are not useful, as they can be when used thoughtfully to enhance the ability to communicate and collaborate concerning student intervention, support, and monitoring progress. Simply stated, label or assign a term to specific performance, along with the specific necessary supportive interventions and supports, rather than label Alexa generally as being a certain way.

When thinking about Alexa, a complex profile of a young lady emerges that can help guide ways to build on her strengths and better address her learning needs. This approach to organizing thinking can help inform with ways in which to organize a coherent set of targeted approaches to help Alexa. More precisely, it appears that Alexa is responding sufficiently well to the universal approaches being applied in the social studies and performing arts classrooms. Furthermore, she appears to be responding sufficiently well (with some additional support from the teacher specific to reading) in her English class and is also making reasonable progress in her Spanish course. However, she clearly is in need of more targeted intervention and instructional support in math and science. As portrayed in Figures 1.1 and 1.2, it would appear that Alexa has some very useful behavioral strengths to build upon in the

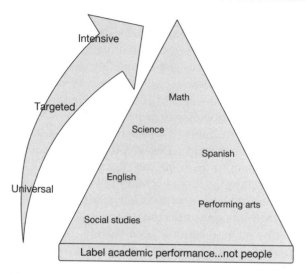

Figure 1.1. Academic levels of need for Alexa. (*Source:* Positive Behavioral Interventions & Supports OSEP Technical Assistance Center; PBIS.org)

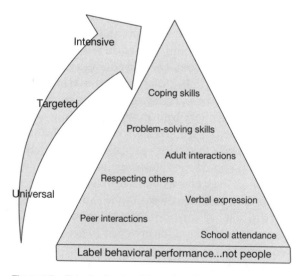

Figure 1.2. Behavioral and social-emotional levels of need for Alexa. (*Source:* Positive Behavioral Interventions & Supports OSEP Technical Assistance Center; PBIS.org)

form of peer interactions; attendance at school; and verbally expressing herself in terms of ideas, wants, and needs. Also, for the most part, she interacts with most adults reasonably well at school. However, Alexa is in clear need of further development of her problem-solving skills and coping skills for use in situations in which she is frustrated (in her case, for use in relation to both math and science).

This description of Alexa's performance is reflective of an MTSS approach, which some schools are employing to organize and deliver instructional practices. This approach supports the organization of integrated targeted academic and behavioral intervention and supports for students such as Alexa. One particular form of an MTSS approach that schools are increasingly employing to organize and deliver behavioral practices is PBIS (Positive Behavioral Interventions and Support OSEP Technical Assistance Center, n.d.). An MTSS approach such as PBIS helps educators to more precisely target and deliver interventions and supports that align to meet the needs of students, such as Alexa, and increases a school's capacity to support the teaching staff to organize and access resources to design and deliver effective instruction. Furthermore, this approach provides a framework within which educators can organize the efficient collection and usage of student performance data to drive decision making.

As mentioned, an MTSS approach typically is organized into three tiers: universal (Tier 1), targeted (Tier 2), and

> Multi-tiered systems of support (MTSS) form a framework for instructional and behavioral support practices, typically organizing practices into 1) universal strategies to offer all students, 2) targeted strategies for some students, and 3) individualized strategies for a few students in greatest need.

individual intensive (Tier 3). Sometimes, these three tiers are described as primary, secondary (or supplemental), and tertiary, respectively. Within this approach, Alexa should not be viewed as a "Tier 2 student." Rather, Alexa should be viewed as a student who is responding sufficiently well to universal (Tier 1) approaches in most areas of learning but who is also in need of targeted (Tier 2) supports to develop problem-solving and coping skills for her use at school (and particularly in math and science). Teaching Alexa problem-solving and coping skills would be further bolstered when delivered in tandem with targeted academic supports specific to both math and science. Thus, Alexa does not fit neatly into a given box, such as exclusively in any one level or tier. She appears to not be sufficiently responding to universal approaches in the math and science classroom; therefore, she is in need of targeted interventions and supports in this regard (but only in this regard).

This example of Alexa provides just one illustration of an MTSS approach to addressing academic and behavioral concerns. This is *not* to suggest that all student profiles will be similar to Alexa's profile. We have used Alexa's example at this time to simply orient you to this way of thinking in order to set the stage for your further reading. The key points right now are as follows:

1. Academic and behavioral learning and performance are interrelated. An attempt to parse out "academic" versus "behavioral" strategies may not be sufficiently helpful.

2. Educators can and should use labels to describe performance and to align interventions and supports to address student needs. However, they should not label students such as Alexa as exclusively fitting into one given level or tier (e.g., a "Tier 2 student").

3. Students are complex, with varying strengths and weaknesses that should be considered as interventions and supports are organized.

Additional Examples Involving Students Who May Benefit from Targeted Supports

Let's look at four more brief examples of student profiles to further illustrate some common characteristics of students who may benefit from targeted interventions and supports. We will return to these student examples in detail in later chapters.

Samuel

According to his third-grade teacher, Samuel is a hands-on learner. He really enjoys and does well with activities involving fine and gross motor skills. Over the past month, Samuel has increasingly required redirection from the teacher and adult volunteer in the classroom during instruction. Samuel has also recently become more physically aggressive, pushing peers on the playground and throwing temper tantrums (crying and screaming) when upset. However, Samuel excels at helping to resolve conflicts between his classmates when they arise (as long as the conflict does not directly involve him). The pattern of these behaviors has been increasing to the point that the teacher can no longer ignore the misbehavior when it occurs in the classroom, as it is becoming unsettling to the other students.

Samuel is unusually tall and athletic compared to his classmates. Samuel's reading level has been measured at 8 months below his grade level, and he also struggles with math concepts. He performs very well in and enjoys art, music, and physical education (PE)—that is, classes that involve other teachers and are referred to as "specials" in his school. He sometimes is disruptive during the social studies and science blocks of instruction; however, he is making reasonable progress in those subject areas. Samuel appears to excel in group activities when he can be a leader but has difficulties with cooperative, noncompetitive play when another classmate is the designated leader (Figures 1.3 and 1.4).

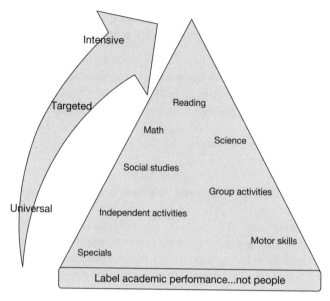

Figure 1.3. Academic levels of need for Samuel. (*Source:* Positive Behavioral Interventions & Supports OSEP Technical Assistance Center; PBIS.org)

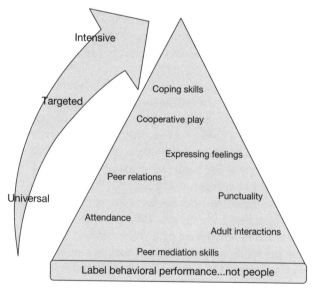

Figure 1.4. Behavioral and social-emotional levels of need for Samuel. (*Source:* Positive Behavioral Interventions & Supports OSEP Technical Assistance Center; PBIS.org)

Selina

Selina is a sixth-grade student who has always flown somewhat under the radar. She appears to be painfully shy, keeps to herself, and has never been known to act disrespectfully towards teachers or peers at school, even when classmates have directed less-than-kind comments toward her. Her academic performance across all of her courses is reasonably steady in the middle of the pack. She clearly prefers to work independently; according to her teachers, there is a noticeable change in her affect and body language when placed in group activities. Selina will respond to questions when asked by peers and teachers during class, but she rarely raises her hand or volunteers at school.

Although Selina possesses the appropriate social skills to interact with her peers in the classroom, she appears to be very distant from her classmates and not interested in common interests among her classmates. For example, only one of her teachers could describe any of Selina's interests outside of school, and that one teacher relayed that it was something she overhead from other students who were talking about Selina in Selina's absence. Selina appears clean and well kept but dresses differently than most of the other girls in sixth grade; she typically wears long-sleeved shirts and tops to school, even on very hot days. In addition, Selina often asks to go to the nurse's office during class time; when she gets there, she typically needs to use the restroom multiple times and then lies down and sleeps. This pattern has been increasing for some time (Figures 1.5 and 1.6).

Julie

Julie is a 10th-grade student and is very involved in a number of school activities. She is a leader in student council, plays two sports, is the captain of the lacrosse team, is in the theatrical stage group, and is involved with numerous volunteer organizations at school. Her academic performance across all coursework is outstanding, and she is involved with the

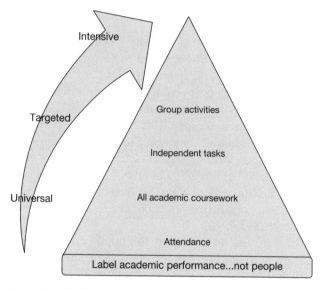

Figure 1.5. Academic levels of need for Selina. (*Source:* Positive Behavioral Interventions & Supports OSEP Technical Assistance Center; PBIS.org)

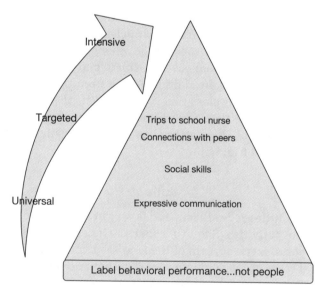

Figure 1.6. Behavioral and social-emotional levels of need for Selina. (*Source:* Positive Behavioral Interventions & Supports OSEP Technical Assistance Center; PBIS.org)

honors program. Julie is a student who teachers love having in class, and she carries a lot of social leverage with peers. She is a high achiever and really goes the extra mile to please others.

Julie recently confided in one of her best friends and one of her teachers (after prompting from her friend) that she is increasingly feeling overwhelmed and stressed to the point of feeling out of control. She shared that she only sleeps 3 or 4 hours a night. She has difficulty falling asleep because there is so much to do; when she does sleep, she often wakes up long before dawn to finish things that she feels she must complete before heading off to school (she does try to sleep most of the day on Sunday to catch up on rest). She is increasingly feeling further stressed about what others will think if her grades or performance slip. Julie admits that she is her own worst critic and that she has to learn to say "no" sometimes. However, she fears losing her status on many levels with others, including her parents, classmates, and teachers (Figures 1.7 and 1.8).

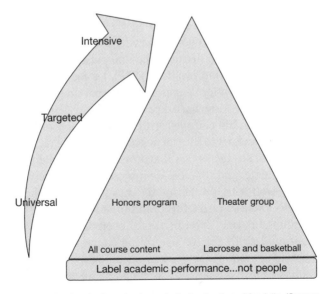

Figure 1.7. Academic and extracurricular levels of need for Julie. (*Source:* Positive Behavioral Interventions & Supports OSEP Technical Assistance Center; PBIS.org)

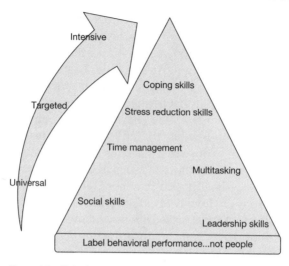

Figure 1.8. Behavioral and social-emotional levels of need for Julie. (*Source:* Positive Behavioral Interventions & Supports OSEP Technical Assistance Center; PBIS.org)

Tyler

Tyler is an 11th-grade student who eagerly discusses his interest in cars and racing with anyone who will listen. He is identified as having an emotional disturbance and subsequently has an individualized education program (IEP). Using varying types of academic and behavioral supports, Tyler participates in most general education coursework. For the most part, he is reasonably successful in his courses, with the exception of physical education (PE) and art to a lesser degree. He is doing very well in math and social studies and is also progressing sufficiently well in English, music, and science. He interacts, for the most part, remarkably well with his classmates throughout the school day and has developed some useful communication skills.

Through his IEP, Tyler has also developed some effective organizational skills for his use in his courses. However, his inconsistent compliance with class-specific expectations in PE and art has him in jeopardy of earning failing grades in those classes. Tyler has been sent to the office on three occasions this year from PE for noncompliance. According to his PE teacher, when Tyler does not want to do something, such as climb a rope in gym class, no one can make him (Figures 1.9 and 1.10).

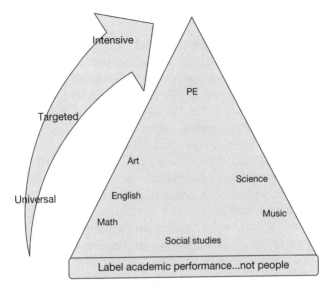

Figure 1.9. Academic levels of need for Tyler. (*Key:* PE, physical education.) (*Source:* Positive Behavioral Interventions & Supports OSEP Technical Assistance Center; PBIS.org)

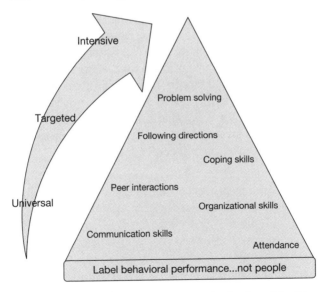

Figure 1.10. Behavioral and social-emotional levels of need for Tyler. (*Source:* Positive Behavioral Interventions & Supports OSEP Technical Assistance Center; PBIS.org)

CONCLUSION

The brief profiles of Alexa, Samuel, Selina, Julie, and Tyler have been provided to help you to understand some of the diverse characteristics of students who may be in need of targeted interventions and supports, as we describe in the following chapters. However, these profiles do not sufficiently describe all of the relevant details associated with each of these students, their classrooms, or their school environments. In light of the limitations of these profiles—and to reiterate the notion of having a solid foundation upon which to build effective practice in the classroom—we want to re-emphasize the importance of implementing universal approaches with fidelity (i.e., as designed to be implemented) in the classroom.

Establishing a safe and efficient classroom environment provides a foundation of universal approaches on which you can layer targeted interventions and support when needed, as we describe in the following chapters. Furthermore, establishing a conducive classroom climate for learning through application of universal approaches helps to minimize the likelihood of students inaccurately appearing in need of intervention and support at advanced tiers (what has sometimes been referred to as "false positives"). Finally, having a foundation of effective universal prevention in the classroom also sets the stage for greater confidence in the use of student performance data to identify students in need of targeted interventions and supports. In Chapter 2, we examine these targeted intervention and support strategies, as well as how one goes about layering them on top of the universal approaches.

2

What Is Targeted Support, and What Does It Mean to Provide Such Support in the Classroom?

Targeted supports can be used with students who do not sufficiently respond to your universal prevention approaches (as part of classroom management, described in Chapter 1). Targeted (Tier 2) approaches are not implemented in place of universal preventive approaches. Rather, they are layered on top of universal prevention (Tier 1) procedures. Layering on targeted support is both logical and relevant whether you are teaching in a PBIS school or a more traditional school setting.

One of the hallmarks of targeted approaches is the increased use of progress monitoring in tandem with establishing procedures to modify interventions and supports as needed with the student(s) of concern. Any type of targeted strategy or modification that is implemented should have

> Implementation of universal preventive approaches will position you to "work smarter" as you layer on needed targeted approaches.

provisions for the gradual decrease or tapering of the targeted intervention and support as your student experiences increasing degrees of success over time. To determine whether your student is indeed experiencing increased success, frequent progress monitoring (including data collection and analysis) is an essential aspect of targeted approaches. Your progress monitoring procedures should efficiently fit in your classroom, like your hand into a glove, given implementation of preventative classroom management (as described in Chapter 1).

In addition to increased progress monitoring, another hallmark of Tier 2 approaches is reclarification and reteaching of expectations along with increased positive reinforcement of the student for meeting the performance expectations that you have already established within your classroom. You should not alter or "dumb down" the behavioral expectations in your classroom as a way of providing targeted supports. Rather, Tier 2 approaches are simply targeted interventions and supports that are reflective of increased data-based instructional practices to support student achievement of the same behavioral competencies that you have already established for all students in your classroom. In other words, it is just as important for students receiving targeted interventions and supports—such as Alexa, Samuel, Selina, Julie, or Tyler (introduced in Chapter 1)—to meet classroom expectations as it is for any of their classmates. Some additional key interrelated features of Tier 2 approaches are described in Table 2.1.

Table 2.1. Interrelated features of targeted supports

Feature	Description
Social skills emphasis	Social skills, like academic skills, require direct instruction. Proactive teaching of social skills (e.g., materials sharing during a project, problem solving associated with resolving a conflict through nonphysical means) should be built in to the ebb and flow of instruction. This instruction is layered on top of, but not in place of, instruction in social skills that occurs with initially teaching behavioral expectations to all students as a part of universal prevention.
Systematic prompting	Prompts come in various forms, including self-monitoring and evaluation cards, verbal reminders and/or physical gestures. Ideally, for consistency, it is valuable to use some form of a point system along with cards for recording, as this tends to enhance student responses to targeted supports.
Opportunities to practice and receive feedback	As with any form of learning, providing students with opportunities to respond is important. Multiple opportunities should be provided throughout the typical school day for student performance coupled with feedback.
Easy access for students	Students should be able to access targeted supports in a timely manner (typically within 3–5 school days). In the case where multiple targeted supports are to be provided, initial components should be delivered in a timely manner.
Time efficiency for teachers	One key for both fidelity in implementation and sustainability is the degree of additional effort required by teachers and staff. The more the delivery of targeted supports is organized in a way that little to no additional effort by classroom teaching staff is required, the more likely the targeted supports will be provided as designed until faded.
Consistency in approach among all teachers	Students should experience common and predictable interactions with teachers and staff at school. The use of common approaches should enhance student learning as well as time efficiency for all involved in targeted supports.

(continued)

Table 2.1. *(continued)*

Feature	Description
Compatibility with expectations for all students	Targeted supports build (layer) on top of universal approaches. Therefore, the same behavioral expectations as for all students continues to be a common focal point in providing targeted supports.
Ongoing progress monitoring	Increasingly, data are collected and used in providing performance feedback to students receiving targeted supports. Performance data are used to provide feedback to the students, identify patterns, and make program decisions, such as when to fade targeted supports.
Flexibility	Student need drives the organization and delivery of targeted supports. Based on needs as measured through performance, a student should be able to easily move from receiving targeted supports to universal supports (or vice versa) in a time-efficient manner.
Function-based supports for students	Patterns of prior student behavior should be considered when aligning targeted supports for students. Particular types of targeted supports may be more or less useful with students who appear motivated by adult or peer attention when compared to students whose prior problem behavior appears escape motivated.
Adequate resources to implement	A clear array of resources (including staff time) should be organized within a flow chart that depicts the process for student access to targeted supports. This is done to minimize the likelihood of staff needing to scurry about trying to organize resources on the fly during the school day.
Communication with home	Regular communication with responsible adults in the students' homes should be structured within targeted supports. The frequency of interaction will be somewhat dependent on the students' needs and the form of targeted support provided.
Data-based approach to fade supports	Student performance data should drive decision making as to when to make changes in practice, including when to begin to taper targeted supports. The fading of targeted supports should be a part of discussions from the onset of the process.

TYPES OF TARGETED SUPPORTS IN YOUR CLASSROOM

Targeted supports come in different shapes, sizes, and varieties. Most targeted supports fall within one of three types: 1) formally designed supportive interventions delivered by you or other staff in the classroom, 2) formally designed and facilitated supports provided by peers and/or other naturally occurring community resources that are accessible to your classroom, or 3) a combination of student- and staff-delivered supports in concert with other natural supports. You are highly encouraged to incorporate natural supports in tandem with formal supports whenever feasible to enhance sustainability.

What Are Natural Supports?

Informal, naturally occurring supports provided by peers or others within the classroom or community are highly encouraged. Naturally occurring supports tend to be the least disruptive to the typical ebb and flow of classroom activities for everyone; they are often the most easily sustained over time and are useful across a variety of situations and settings. One example of natural support at the most basic level includes one student helping a classmate in an unprompted manner when he or she notices that the classmate is persistently struggling with something (e.g., an academic task, a classroom chore, or another form of task in the classroom). Another example is when an adult volunteer who is assigned to a classroom to support the teacher in working with all students proactively helps a particular child who has a history of struggling with certain assignments. In these two examples, the support emerges from within the classroom as a natural part of the learning environment.

It is important to understand that while naturally occurring supports in many instances may represent the ideal, it is very unlikely that relying exclusively on natural supports will be sufficient as an approach to meet the needs of the particular student(s) in need of targeted supports. We do not share this to discourage your exploration and use of such natural supports.

To the contrary, natural supports are most worthy of pursuit. We simply want to emphasize that you will likely need to initially begin with designing and delivering more formalized types of targeted supports to set the stage for more natural forms of supports to emerge over time in your classroom. As such, it is helpful to think about naturally occurring supports from the onset when planning targeted supports.

Planning Formal Supports

There are two important factors to take into account as you begin to plan formally designed targeted supports. First, it is important to understand that there is a menu of options of targeted supports to consider. Second, the nature of your classroom should influence which approaches on this menu make the most sense for you. Finding the right match—sometimes referred to as *contextual fit*—is important for meeting everyone's needs within your classroom.

You likely have a broad array of targeted support options from which to select if you are teaching within a PBIS school. However, there are likely targeted support options if you are teaching within a school that has not formally established PBIS or similar multi-tiered systems of support, although they are typically fewer and perhaps more cumbersome for you as a classroom teacher to access. Therefore, the first step is to complete *resource mapping* of the available targeted supports in your school. Your resource map should identify the name of the targeted supports that are available in your school, a brief description of the supports, the name of a contact person who organizes each of the targeted supports, and a brief description of the supports available to you as the classroom teacher. Table 2.2 provides an example of a partially completed resource map in PBIS schools as well as more traditional school programs. This table can serve as a first step when making your list or map of the supports and resources at your disposal.

Table 2.2. Key examples of targeted supports via resource mapping

Name of available targeted support	Description of available targeted support for the student(s)	Contact person who organizes the targeted support	Description of supports for the classroom teacher
Example in PBIS school: Behavior Education Program (BEP; Crone, Horner & Hawken, 2004)—also known as Check-In/ Check-Out (CICO)	This approach is designed for students with reoccurring behavioral problems that are not considered dangerous. Students carry with them a daily progress report (DPR) card to and from each class they go to during the day. The student and teacher(s) independently rate the student's performance during the class period at the end of each class period. A check-in and checkout meeting occurs at predetermined times on a daily basis with his or her assigned staff member (typically not the classroom teacher, although it could be depending on how the school organizes this form of targeted support), with the assigned staff member providing feedback/ encouragement to the student as well as documenting performance. Parents are encouraged to participate by signing off on DPRs when brought home by their child that same evening (and, in turn, the student brings the signed DPR back the next school day).	Designated Tier 2 team staff	Provides a structured framework for increasing the degree of positive reinforcement for the student meeting behavioral expectations (through frequent measures) as well as increased opportunities for constructive student–adult interactions (through the check-in and checkout meetings). DPRs (the actual cards) are standardized and already developed, and the assigned staff member who holds the check-in and checkout meetings with the student represents an additional resource to the classroom teacher. The emphasis on the DPRs can be academic, behavioral, or a combination of both. Progress monitoring data are collected through the process for review and analysis by the targeted support (Tier 2) team in the building reflective of classroom teacher input/ perspective, which is used to make instructional decisions.

(continued)

Table 2.2. *(continued)*

Name of available targeted support	Description of available targeted support for the student(s)	Contact person who organizes the targeted support	Description of supports for the classroom teacher
Example in traditional school: individual teacher-adapted version of the BEP—also known as CICO	This approach is designed for students with reoccurring behavioral problems that are not considered dangerous. Students check in and check out at predetermined times on a daily basis with the classroom teacher (e.g., homeroom, end of last period during the school day), documenting performance on a student-specific Behavior Progress Report (BPR). The teacher selects a manageable time interval for evaluation of student performance relevant to the amount of time the teacher is instructing the student on a daily basis (e.g., a primary grade teacher may decide to check in several times through each school day, whereas a middle school teacher might conduct a check-in meeting on a less frequent	Classroom teacher	All materials (e.g., BPR card) and procedures are designed and implemented by the classroom teacher. This provides a structured framework for increasing the degree of positive reinforcement for the student meeting behavioral expectations (through structured measures) as well as increased opportunities for constructive student–adult interactions (through the check-in and checkout meetings). The emphasis on the BPRs can be academic, behavioral, or a combination of both. Progress monitoring data are collected through the process for review and analysis by the classroom teacher, which is used to make instructional decisions.

basis due to limited access to the student outside of the scheduled class period). Feedback and encouragement are provided during check-in and checkout sessions by the classroom teacher in addition to the typical degree of feedback and encouragement provided within the ebb and flow of the instructional day (e.g., using the previous example, a primary grade teacher may have the capacity to hold a checkout meeting on a daily basis as a result of having four measures daily, whereas a middle school teacher may hold a checkout meeting at the end of each week given that teacher only sees the student for one period per day). Parents are encouraged to participate by signing off on BPRs when brought home by their child that same evening (and, in turn, the student brings the signed BPR back the next school day to the classroom teacher regardless of the frequency of the checkout meeting).

Source: Crone, Horner, and Hawken (2004).

Targeted (Tier 2)
Supports within PBIS Schools

One valuable resource to build upon is an established data collection system, which should already be in place if you are working within a PBIS school (e.g., School-wide Information System, or SWIS; May et al., 2000). Using your school's data system can help you to identify students who appear to be in need of targeted supports, which in turn can help you get these students quicker access to targeted supports. Beyond the use of discipline referrals, other examples of useful data sources include attendance and tardiness records (including visits to the school nurse), completion of credit hours towards graduation, performance on high-stakes testing required for graduation at the secondary level, and work/course completion (including grades) across all grade levels. Consideration of already available information sets the stage for the selection of particular targeted supports to address identified needs. A number of targeted supports are commonly available within PBIS schools.

Check and Connect   One example of a targeted support that is commonly available in PBIS schools is known as Check and Connect (Sinclair et al., 1998). In Check and Connect, an identified staff member (usually *not* a given student's classroom teacher) serves as a primary point of contact for the student of concern. This person may perform many important duties, including meeting with the student on a periodic basis and serving as a liaison between the student and members of his or her family as well as relevant staff at school, staff from other child-serving agencies, and people who may be able to provide natural support at school or in the local community. PBIS schools implementing Check and Connect typically establish two levels of operations, often referred to as *basic* and *intensive.* The basic level features the assigned staff member meeting with the student on a periodic but less frequent basis (e.g., perhaps once a month) as compared to more frequent meetings and interactions at the intensive level. Meetings typically focus on progress updates on school performance and applying problem-solving approaches. Direct review and reteaching of social skills are also commonly part of Check and Connect.

> Check and Connect consists of regular meetings between an adult and the student, primarily to help the student improve problem-solving techniques and social skills.

Talk with a member of your PBIS Leadership Team (or your school administrator) about how to access Check and Connect if your school has established this as one of your targeted support programs. Check and Connect can be particularly helpful in improving performance by students whose behavior appears to be attention motivated because it provides an appropriate avenue for extra adult attention. We have provided references in the Resources for more information about this specific approach.

The Behavior Education Program (Check-In/Check-Out)

Another targeted support typically available on the menu of options in PBIS schools is the Behavior Education Program (BEP; Crone et al., 2004), which is referred to in many schools as Check-In/Check-Out (CICO). This program has been shown to be helpful in improving student performance across behavioral functions (although it is generally considered more effective for attention-seeking rather than escape-motivated behaviors). Like the Check and Connect approach, CICO emphasizes scheduled meetings with the student of concern. However, CICO is organized around frequent, scheduled meetings on a daily basis.

Most schools implementing CICO identify a common staff member (often a paraprofessional) with whom the student checks in at the start of the school day and checks out at the end of the day. These meetings are usually just a few minutes in duration. Check-in meetings typically focus on preparedness and initial encouragement for the school day (e.g., check

> Check-In/Check-Out (CICO) consists of more frequent meetings, often helping a student stay organized and attuned to how he or she is doing at meeting schoolwide and classroom expectations throughout the day.

homework, provide the student with a daily progress report to present to teachers upon entry to each respective classroom throughout the day, give some words of encouragement). Checkout meetings mostly focus on tallying the daily points earned by the student (keeping in mind that the daily progress reports focus on schoolwide expectations, which also should be consistent with your classroom expectations), as well as the delivery of additional acknowledgment for performance, guidance, and encouragement. Furthermore, there is a home communication element to CICO, in which the student brings the daily progress report home for review (and in many instances, parent signature). We encourage you to use this form of targeted support if it is on your school's menu of options. We have also provided you with some references for CICO in the Resources for additional information.

Some PBIS schools actually provide both Check and Connect and CICO to support their students. In such instances, Check and Connect (basic level) may serve as the initial form of targeted support provided, with CICO reserved for implementation if or when the student of concern does not sufficiently respond to Check and Connect. This arrangement is both logical and consistent with the overall organizational framework of PBIS. Again, we encourage you to consider using Check and Connect and/or CICO depending on the menu of targeted supports available at your school.

Targeted Social Skills Training   An additional targeted approach that is also commonly available in PBIS schools is targeted social skills training. In many instances, students are scheduled for reteaching activities associated with schoolwide and classroom expectations. Social skills instruction may already be occurring as a part of universal approaches at your school, but as a targeted strategy, this provides a data-based way to bring a small group of students (who appear to need it) together for additional instruction and feedback. Schools tend to go about organizing the reteaching sessions in a variety of ways. As such, this means that you as the teacher of record for a given student receiving targeted support may (or may not) have direct involvement in delivering these additional small-group sessions. However, at a minimum, as the classroom teacher you should be in the loop of information and providing guidance and feedback to your student on an ongoing basis in your classroom.

Mentoring   Mentoring represents yet another targeted approach that has been implemented in school systems with success. As with the previously described targeted supports, the foundation of mentoring is in fostering connectedness within the school and ideally in the community. Mentoring, in a unique manner, also often tends to further foster more naturally occurring support systems for students in both the school and community, although such effects are somewhat dependent on how the mentoring program is designed. In our experience, rarely should a mentoring program serve as the only formally designed targeted approach. However, mentoring programs are often incorporated as a part of an array of targeted approaches (e.g., mentoring in tandem with Check and Connect).

Mentors may be adults, older students, or interested peers. Schools that have employed mentoring approaches may work with established mentoring initiatives (e.g., Big Brothers Big Sisters) or develop their own procedures, typically through collaboration with local community resources (e.g., a local college or university). As with the targeted approaches previously described, as a classroom teacher in a PBIS school, you will want to make sure you are aware and connected with the mentoring options that your school may provide.

PBIS as a Support for You

> You are *not* alone when trying to layer on targeted supports with a particular student in your classroom within a PBIS school.

What is very evident about targeted supports in a PBIS school is that you, as the teacher trying to effectively work with a student who is not sufficiently responding to your universal classroom approaches, are not working alone with the student of concern. Check and Connect, CICO, targeted social skills instruction, and mentoring programs are collaborative endeavors commonly present within a PBIS school. Thus, your administrator or PBIS team should be able to guide and support you in these endeavors. In other words, you should not be on your own trying to layer on targeted supports with a particular student in your classroom within a PBIS school.

Targeted (Tier 2) Supports within Traditional Schools

Although you may not have access to the full benefits associated with the collaborative options of targeted approaches commonly available in PBIS schools (e.g., CICO), there are likely still options for you to consider in a more traditional school. First, because there may not be standardized procedures in place for identifying students in need of targeted supports, it is likely that you may identify a given student based on your intuitive sense of how he or she is responding in your classroom. Obviously, your use of intuition alone may not be as reliable as documentation such as discipline referrals, but at the start, your intuitive sense may likely serve as the most readily available information in your classroom. Also, although there may not be a formalized menu of supports at your school, most traditional schools do have, in their own way, some array of well-intended targeted supports (e.g., mentoring programs). Unfortunately, without proper organization and despite good intent, such initiatives and resources can appear disjointed and difficult to access. It is much more work for frontline folks—such as you, the classroom teacher—to try to navigate the array of resources without the benefit of a clear and explicit protocol that is organized into a multi-tiered framework. Further, targeted supports in traditional schools tend to require the classroom teacher to take on most of the heavy lifting to address the needs of a particular student, which may not be sustainable over time. To be clear, we are not suggesting that continued overreliance on you as the teacher taking on increasing degrees of workload is by design in most traditional schools. Rather, it simply can become a byproduct (despite intentions to the contrary) when schools lack a coherent multi-tiered organizational framework.

Behavior Progress Reports One targeted support worth exploration in your classroom may be an adaptation of the use of daily progress reports from the Behavior Education Program (CICO). We suggest starting with an adaptation of this approach because it provides you with a reasonably efficient form of targeted support that should be within your direct reach or ability to implement. To help keep things clear and to distinguish daily progress reports (DPRs) associated with CICO from the adapted application we are suggesting here, we will refer to this adapted approach as Behavior Progress Reports (BPRs). We have also provided some examples of BPRs for your convenience in the Appendix.

First, you should target what you believe to be a reasonable length of time or interval for use of this adapted approach. Daily progress reports associated with CICO (as previously described) reflect the student's behavior based on a daily time frame. However, there are typically multiple measures that occur with CICO within a given school day as the student goes from class to class (e.g., three measures in the morning and three in the afternoon plus the lunch period, resulting in seven measures in a given day). Application of CICO requires the infrastructure of coordination that comes with multi-tiered systems of support (e.g., PBIS) because multiple staff may be involved in the process in partnership with the student. In a more traditional school, due to time constraints, you may need to start with fewer measures in a given day and, in turn, debrief with your student on a less frequent basis so that you can consistently implement and sustain the targeted support over time (e.g., in a second-grade classroom, perhaps one morning and one afternoon measure per day and meeting to review progress once or twice per week).

To be clear, we are not suggesting that such an adapted approach will be as precise, effective, or efficient as systematic application of DPRs within CICO, but it is a logical place to start if you do not have access to additional supports to run high-fidelity CICO. Applying BPRs as described will provide you with a practical approach that reflects increased progress monitoring with your student. You can adjust the frequency of measures and debriefing sessions as appropriate based on student progress (or lack of a sufficient rate of progress) as well as other factors in your classroom (e.g., your time and energy). Also of great importance, please remember that you are encouraged to continue application of your universal classroom approaches, as described in Chapter 1, in tandem with layering on your use of BPRs as needed.

> Behavior progress reports can provide a good starting point for targeted supports if your school is not implementing PBIS.

Behavior Contracts   In the event that your student does not sufficiently respond to your use of BPRs, you may need to consider a behavior contract. There are two important things to keep in mind from our perspective when developing a behavior contract. First, the primary goal of a behavior contract is to see sufficient improvement in behavior so that you can wean the student off the contract within a reasonable time frame. Second, what a behavior contract entails is at its core simply a more systematic, student-centered way of further defining, reteaching, and reinforcing behavioral expectations to increase the likelihood of your student doing things the correct way. An effective behavior contract should position you to reinforce your student for desired behavior at a more sufficient rate based on performance. This is typically accomplished by further operationally defining the universal behavioral expectations that you have already established in your classroom while also establishing a clear criterion for performance within a reasonable (typically shorter) time interval for that given student. An effective behavior contract has more to do with reinforcement procedures for appropriate behavior than it has to do with negative responses to inappropriate behavior (given, of course, that you select a reasonable time interval for measurement along with meaningful reinforcement procedures for the student).

> A behavior contract is nothing more than a way of defining, reteaching, and reinforcing behavioral expectations to increase the likelihood of your student doing things the correct way.

One of the more confusing aspects of establishing a behavior contract with a student can be the selection of your time interval for measurement. On the surface, this may seem like a simple thing to do. However, the identification of the time interval must not be an arbitrary choice. Rather, you are encouraged to think about how often the student engages in problem behavior that requires redirection prior to implementation of the behavior contract (also known as the baseline of occurrence of the problem behavior). Then, using this number (the baseline in a given day and/or class period), you can target time intervals that will better position you (as the teacher) to achieve the 4:1 ratio of reinforcement to correction (see Table 1.1).

For example, let's say that the baseline of an eighth-grade student disrupting his classmates from completing their work during independent work time averages one class session per week for a class that convenes for five sessions per week. Using the entire class period as the initial time interval enables the 4:1 ratio to be achieved over the course of the week; for four class periods per week, the student should initially be successful, on task, and working quietly, whereas the student might fail to meet this expectation in one class period. Criteria for performance may be changed over time as the student is successful, resulting in renegotiation of the contract. The time interval selected will need to reflect relevant information regarding the performance of your student of concern and the logistics of your classroom operations. A few examples of behavior contracts are provided in Chapter 5 for your review.

Mentoring   Beyond use of BPRs and behavior contracts, it is certainly appropriate to consider the use of some form of mentoring program as previously described. In fact, such noncontingent attention (e.g., personal interactions) can be a powerful way of building rapport. Connecting your student with an adult or older peer of his or her preference to provide periodic support and guidance can help to reduce problem behavior. There is a broad array of ways in which teachers have established mentoring programs. Common across effective mentoring programs are one-to-one mentor-mentee interactions over the course of time. The time necessary to establish a reasonable degree of rapport between the mentor and mentee will vary based on many factors. Initially, it is helpful to engage in high-frequency contact (e.g., between 2 and 5 minutes per day for at least 5–10 consecutive days) and to focus on "safe" topics for conversation, such as student interests rather than school difficulties. Mentoring programs may be used in tandem with BPRs as well as a behavior contract.

Talking About PBIS with Your School

In our experience, schools that have MTSS tend to have greater natural capacity to support teachers in meeting the needs of students who require targeted supports. Obviously, having access to existent resources at your school to support your endeavors in applying targeted supports is advantageous to you as a teacher. Similarly, having school resources available that facilitate your use of evidenced-based instructional practices (e.g., student choice of task sequence when appropriate, task variation, providing sufficient opportunities for student responses) also can make it easier for your classroom to work effectively. In light of this reality, we highly encourage you to concurrently engage colleagues at your school in discussions about establishing MTSS (e.g., PBIS). There is rarely a convenient time to initiate these types of conversations during a school year, but we believe it is essential to have these discussions in order to build such capacity in your school system.

> As a step toward longer-term capacity building, talk with your colleagues and administrators about establishing multi-tiered systems of support (MTSS; e.g., PBIS).

TARGETED SUPPORTS
AND INTERNALIZING BEHAVIORS

Most of the scientific support for the targeted supports described in this book (and PBIS at the universal level as well) has historically emphasized measurement associated with externalizing forms of behavioral challenges (e.g., office discipline referrals). However, often students who exhibit visible problem behavior may also have internalizing conditions, and targeted supports can be very helpful for these students as well as those with externalizing concerns. It has been argued that internalizing behavior is the over control of feelings (emotions) and can be thought to fall into four general categories: anxiety, depression, social withdrawal, and somatic complaints. Sound implementation of targeted supports can prove particularly helpful to further build resiliency in these students at the same time as increasing prosocial behavior at school.

Students in your classroom who may have internalizing conditions, such as social withdrawal or an anxiety disorder, may also benefit from the general improvement in the classroom climate as a result of delivery of targeted supports to other students with externalizing behavior in your classroom. Everyone in a given classroom will easily notice a student who acts out; subsequently, that particular student's actions (e.g., yelling at others) certainly affects the perceptions and feelings of the other students as well as you, as the teacher in the classroom. For example, suppose a particular student has a history of making derogatory comments towards other students in your classroom. Some of the other students in your classroom may be able to successfully cope and ignore this student's problem behavior when it does occur. However, it is very likely that certain students will have greater difficulty in this regard, and the stress created by this other student's actions may actually impede a few students' ability to perform in your classroom.

Taking this one step further, perhaps for a student or two in this smaller group of students, the stress induced through continuous exposure to being called names by this other student may trigger feelings of concern for safety or resurface traumatic memories that may cause those particular students to shut down. Students with internalizing conditions tend to benefit from trauma-informed classroom environments where teachers proactively build prosocial skills. Sound implementation of both universal and targeted supports can help to create a more conducive learning environment for all of your students. Such a learning environment is supportive to your students receiving targeted supports as well as their classmates—and certainly for you as the teacher!

CONCLUSION

In summary, the brief descriptions of targeted supports provided in this chapter serve as a prelude to later chapters, in which we provide more explicit descriptions and guidance along with illustrations across PBIS and traditional schools. Regardless of the type of school within which you are teaching, one consistent theme with targeted supports is increased progress monitoring of student performance—more specifically, gathering and utilizing student performance data to inform your practice in your classroom. Yes, we used that nasty four letter word—*data*. Being teachers ourselves, we completely understand your potential adverse reaction to that word. We also understand firsthand the big difference between functional data that a teacher gathers to inform instruction as opposed to data that someone else has told us as teachers that we have to collect. In light of this understanding, in Chapter 3, we share with you what we believe to be the most efficient, practical, and pragmatic approaches to organize data collection associated with targeted supports for use in your classroom.

3

How Do I Gather Practical Information on Student Behavior in My Classroom?

The collection of data helps to provide targeted supports because it gives teachers tangible information to share and use to inform their practice. Data are collected for a number of reasons, including screening and progress monitoring purposes. For example, behavioral screeners provide information to help with the early identification of students who may require targeted supports. When students who are not sufficiently responding to universal prevention are identified sooner rather than later, teachers have the opportunity to provide targeted support in a time-efficient manner. Beyond screening for students in need of targeted supports, continued collection and analysis of data are used to monitor progress on how students are responding to targeted supports. Progress monitoring is a way of keeping tabs on whether a support strategy appears to be effective and if it continues to be needed.

SCREENING TO ESTABLISH THE NEED FOR TIER 2 SUPPORT WITHIN PBIS SCHOOLS

The use of data occurs early and often within a PBIS school. A systematic screening process is typically established to identify students who are not responding sufficiently to universal prevention. Screening often occurs throughout the school year (e.g., monthly, seasonally) and can reflect a combination of methods. Screening methods include nomination from teachers, administrators, students, or parents, a review of student behavior data (e.g., office disciplinary referrals, attendance, visits to school nurse), analysis of student scores on standardized behavior screening instruments (e.g., Student Risk Screening Scale–Teacher [SRSS-T; Drummond, 1994]), and a review of student academic data. Because there are so many sources of data and timing can differ as to when they are available, PBIS schools are encouraged to create an assessment schedule grid. The use of this grid, which reflects schoolwide data sources, helps to ensure that a wide variety of tools are used, that accurate information is obtained, that a person is responsible for monitoring each type of data, and that time is set aside to analyze and interpret data to inform practice. Other important factors typically considered in a PBIS school in relation to this grid include whether the data gathering approaches are practical for staff, whether a timely response can be provided to needs as they emerge, and whether there is flexibility in the procedures. Specific to screening to help identify students for targeted supports, it is important to establish a specific cutoff score that you and your colleagues can use in the process of qualifying a student for targeted supports. Table 3.1 provides an example of an assessment schedule grid in PBIS schools, including sample criteria for targeting students for supports. To provide further context, the following sections detail some of the previously indicated potential screening methods.

Teacher Nomination

One common screening approach is for teachers to nominate students of concern (e.g., students who are not sufficiently responding

Table 3.1. Example of assessment schedule grid showing various data collection methods

Types of data collection	Who typically collects the data?	How often?	What criteria indicate the need for targeted support?
Teacher nomination	Administrators or teachers	Sought twice per year	Nomination by teacher and substantiated by an additional method or another staff member
Student attendance	Office staff	Collected daily; reported to staff quarterly	More than four absences by mid-year
Student office discipline referral (ODR)	Office staff or Tier 2 team member	Collected daily; reported to staff quarterly	Two or more ODRs by mid-year
Student grades	Teachers	Reported to administrators quarterly	Grade of D or lower in two or more courses
Formal screeners	Administrators	Administered three times per year	Student's score falls within the at-risk range

Source: Lane, Kalberg, and Menzies (2009).

to universal prevention). For example, you may be asked to nominate up to three students in your classroom who require multiple reminders from you to meet expectations during a typical day, are getting these reminders across settings (e.g., in expressive arts, in content areas, and during lunch or recess), and have been referred to the office due to problem behavior on more than one occasion. Nominations also can be considered for other potential concerns, such as significant changes in student demeanor or health-related issues (e.g., increasing visits to the school nurse).

Office Discipline Referrals

Office discipline referral (ODR) data are commonly used in PBIS schools to identify students who are not sufficiently responding to universal supports. To meaningfully use ODR data, it is important to operationally define infractions and clearly denote the circumstances associated with referrals. For example, as a teacher in a PBIS school, you may use the School-wide Information System (SWIS; May et al., 2000), a suite of web-based software applications, to manage the ODR data. SWIS provides a way to more easily record information about each referral and to review groups of ODR data to analyze behavior patterns. Teachers in schools using SWIS still must create operational definitions and decision-making rules to determine which behaviors warrant referral. Annual teacher training is provided to help teachers distinguish between nuisance behaviors and problem behaviors that warrant referral.

Standardized Behavior Screening Instruments

Behavioral screeners can also help to determine students who may benefit from targeted supports. When choosing a behavioral screener, the instrument should have strong psychometric properties, such as validity and reliability (meaning that the screener measures what you intend to measure and shows consistency over time), and should be feasible and reasonable to administer. Some of the more commonly used screeners for identifying students in need of targeted support in early childhood through secondary PBIS schools are depicted in Table 3.2.

As teachers well know, you do not have to go looking under the proverbial rocks in the classroom to find students who act out (i.e., students who display externalizing behavior); these students tend to be pretty easy to find. However, screening for students with internalizing behavioral concerns can be more challenging. The Systematic Screening for Behavior Disorders (SSBD; Walker & Severson, 1992) may serve as an effective screener to identify students with internalizing behavioral concerns, although it can be labor intensive. The Behavior Intervention Monitoring Assessment System (BIMAS; McDougal, Bardos, & Meier, 2011) may also prove helpful to identify students with internalizing concerns. Short of using a formal screener such as the SSBD or BIMAS,

Table 3.2. Common social-emotional screeners for identifying students in need of targeted support

Screener	Description	Grade	For externalizing or internalizing behaviors?	Related information and links (as of the time of this writing)
BASC-3 (Kamphaus & Reynolds, 2015)	Identifies behavioral and emotional strengths and weaknesses	Pre-K to 12	Both	See http://www.pearsonclinical.com/education/products/100001402/behavior-assessment-system-for-children-third-edition-basc-3.html Is part of the BESS (Kamphaus & Reynolds, 2007)
BERS-2 (Epstein, 2004)	Screens for aggression, interpersonal strength, family involvement, intrapersonal strength, school functioning, and affective strength	K–12	Both	See http://www.proedinc.com/customer/productView.aspx?ID=3430
SSIS (Gresham & Elliot, 2008)	Identifies strengths, performance deficits, acquisition problems, prosocial behavior, motivation, and reading and math skills	Pre-K to 12	Both	See http://www.pearsonclinical.com/education/products/100000322/social-skills-improvement-system-ssis-rating-scales.html
SDQ (Goodman, 1997)	Involves a questionnaire for screening students ages 4–17 years; an early years version covers ages 2–4 years	Pre-K to 10	Internalizing	Available for download at www.sdqinfo.com

(continued)

Table 3.2. *(continued)*

Screener	Description	Grade	For externalizing or internalizing behaviors?	Related information and links (as of the time of this writing)
SRSS (Drummond, 1994)	Uses a seven-item behavioral screening to detect antisocial behavior	K–12	Externalizing	Free access tool available at http://miblsi.cenmi.org/MiBLSiModel/Evaluation/Measures/StudentRiskScreeningScale.aspx
SSBD (Walker & Severson, 1992)	Uses a three-stage multiple-gating to identify students with externalizing or internalizing behaviors	K–6	Both	See http://www.nhcebis.seresc.net/universal_ssbd for more information.
BIMAS (McDougal, Bardos, & Meier, 2011)	Is a 34-item social, emotional, behavioral, and academic tool that can be used for universal screening and assessing response to intervention; is useful for behavioral universal screening, progress monitoring, outcome assessment, and program evaluation within a tiered framework	K–12	Both	Information regarding the screener's use is available via the publisher at http://www.mhs.com/product.aspx?gr=edu&prod=bimas&id=overview

Source: Patel and Runge (2011).

Note: These screeners are commonly used with early childhood through secondary school children. The measures are generally considered reliable and valid.

Key: BASC-3, Behavior Assessment System for Children – Third Edition; BESS, Behavioral and Emotional Screening System; BERS-2, Behavioral and Emotional Rating Scale – Second Edition; SSIS, Social Skills Improvement System; SDQ, Strengths and Difficulties Questionnaire; SRSS, Student Risk Screening Scale; SSBD, Systematic Screening for Behavior Disorders; BIMAS, Behavior Intervention Monitoring Assessment System.

you and your colleagues can look for patterns in behavior through attendance, tardiness, falling grades, or sudden behavioral changes. If you go this route, please remember that these more subjectively interpreted patterns can be misleading at times. Thus, you should be cautious in your interpretations (e.g., not all students with attendance issues have internalizing behavioral concerns).

> Data on behavior and academic progress are reviewed as part of the screening process for selecting students who may benefit from targeted supports.

It is also important to consider academic progress in screening. A few commonly used academic screeners in the area of reading include AIMSweb (NCS Pearson, n.d.), Dynamic Indicators of Basic Early Literacy Skills (DIBELS; Kaminski & Good, 1998), and the Brief Academic Competence Evaluation Screening System (BACESS; Kettler, Elliott, & Albers, 2008). Furthermore, the use of curriculum-based measurement (CBM) and curriculum-based assessment (CBA) can be helpful in monitoring academic progress. More information on these tools can be found in the Resources.

SCREENING TO ESTABLISH THE NEED FOR TARGETED SUPPORTS WITHIN TRADITIONAL SCHOOLS

Data are equally important to you if you teach in a traditional school setting. However, given that the array of data-based decision-making structures may be more limited, you will likely need to create a practical approach to identify students in your classroom who may be at risk and in need of targeted support. In a parallel sense to a PBIS school, you are encouraged to establish a screening process to include nomination by yourself or others, direct observation in your classroom, social-emotional and behavioral screening within your classroom, and other sources of classroom data. In this section, we review each of these approaches in order to understand how to gather this data initially and throughout the year. Some of these approaches are more subjective than others, so having a healthy balance will likely give you the best results.

Teacher and Other Adult Nominations

One place to start is by creating, with the students' parents or previous year teachers, a list of students who may have been eligible or received targeted supports. It may be helpful to ask teachers from the prior year (with permission from the building principal) to rank the top three students that they had in their classrooms in terms of academic, social-emotional, and behavioral needs. In using this approach, it is important to keep in mind that classroom environments may have significant difference. You may also want to talk with your school's guidance counselor along these same lines concerning this type of screening.

Direct Observation

Direct observation can help you monitor behavior in real time in your classroom. A few direct observation methods may be more feasible and easy for you to use. One such approach—using frequency counts—utilizes a tally for each time a behavior of concern occurs. This is commonly used for behaviors that occur often but not so often that they are too cumbersome to count. Frequency data could be used throughout the entire day or sampled for a snapshot of the day (e.g., how many times a student is out of his or her seat in a half-hour period). A second type of direct observation—interval recording—involves recording behavioral occurrence or nonoccurrence using predetermined intervals or blocks of time. For example, you may use a daily checklist for your math block where your class is broken down into three 15-minute intervals to check off whether a behavior has occurred or not occurred within each 15-minute segment of the total 45-minute instructional session. You may, of course, make your block of time longer or shorter than 15 minutes depending on what type of student behavior you wish to measure in your classroom. To make direct observation manageable in your classroom, we also encourage you to explore ways that others can help with the data collection (e.g., paraeducator, community volunteer, co-teacher). A third method of direct observation commonly used in the classroom is anecdotal recording. Anecdotal recording requires you to write a brief summary of the targeted student behavior that was observed throughout the designated timeframe (e.g., course of the day). It is important to be as objective as possible by writing facts (not interpretations or judgments) and record what happened in such a way that you can meaningfully use the information.

> Frequency counts, interval recording, and anecdotal recording can be great approaches for gathering direct observation data in your classroom.

Screening Instruments

When feasible, the use of a social-emotional and behavioral screener combined with direct observation data may provide you with the most complete picture of your students. Therefore, you may want to include a teacher and parent rating scale in your data collection procedures. The Strengths and Difficulties Questionnaire (SDQ; Goodman, 1997) is a useful option to consider because it can be found online (http://www.sdqinfo .com) and includes a teacher, parent, and self-report (student) form.

The Direct Behavior Rating (DBR; Chafouleas, Riley-Tillman, & Christ, 2009) approach is another practical method of screening that combines direct observation and a rating scale. To use this approach, you first define the behavior of concern, then you establish a rating scale with indicators ranging from occurrence to nonoccurrence. For example, to rate Tyler's on-task behavior in PE, you might use a scale ranging from 0 (refusal to participate in class activities and impeding classmates' participation) to 5 (engaged in class activities for the majority of the class period). You should develop clear definitions as to what the behavior of concern looks like for each rating item to be scored between 0 and 5 on the scale. This method may be a feasible way for you to get information about a particular student in your class or even about your class as a whole. For example, if you find that too many of the students in your class are having trouble engaging in expected behavior for the majority of the class period, it may be a sign that your expectations are not clear or that students are not being reinforced sufficiently for positive behavior.

Regardless of how you go about gathering data, it is important to intentionally look for students who may appear to be struggling with internalizing behavioral challenges (e.g., anxiety). As noted previously, internalizing behavioral concerns are not as immediately visible as externalized behaviors. One way for you to note students who may be at risk for internalizing concerns is by reviewing attendance and other school records that track students repeatedly missing school, reported changes in sleep or eating patterns, repeated tardiness, increasing visits to the school nurse, or incomplete work. Although it is important to intentionally look for these students, be cautious: These patterns are not always clear indicators of internalizing conditions. You are encouraged to involve school counselors or the school psychologist in the process of analyzing the data to look for indicators of potential internalizing concerns.

> Consistent and thorough definitions of behaviors are especially critical when multiple people may be collecting and using data.

ORGANIZING YOUR DATA FOR USE

Now that you are familiar with some approaches to data collection in PBIS as well as traditional school settings to identify potential students in need of targeted support, you can consider the use of these same data collection approaches to monitor progress over time. First, create a list of the data collection procedures that you have decided to employ. Also, prioritize the student behaviors that you feel are of greatest concern. Next, think about what priority behavior you are looking to address and clearly define the behavior. Be consistent with terminology and define your terms so they are clear to anyone collecting data. For example, "out-of-seat" behavior could be defined as the student being in a different place than he or she should be at that time as well as being where he or she is supposed to be but standing up. Another example may be defining engagement in class. You may collect information on the engagement of your student of concern and decide to increase engagement as one way to help increase his or her academic performance in a class. You may further define engagement as eyes on the teacher or materials and actively writing, responding, and participating in tasks that are being done in your class at that time. It is important to come up with common terms and definitions that make sense to you as you organize your targeted data collection. For example, you might view a student as being disrespectful when he or she uses inappropriate verbal or body language or statements that are offensive to others. However, the paraeducator in your classroom might view disrespect in another manner. Having a clear, agreed-on definition helps you to reliably and efficiently gather data.

You are encouraged to use more than one data collection method to see a more complete picture of what is happening in your classroom. For example, it would be ideal to have a combination of your direct observation data, data from a formal screener, and information from other teachers who previously had your students in class the last year. However, if you can only obtain one type of data on a consistent basis, use this one source on a consistent basis because quality is more important than quantity.

Next, create a plan for gathering and reporting the data. Identify who will collect the data, when and how the data will be collected (e.g., formal screening tool vs. filling out a DBR on any given day), and who will enter the completed data into your database (e.g., SWIS in a PBIS school, some form of spreadsheet in a more traditional school). This way of organizing—before starting to collect the data—is important for ensuring that you (and your colleagues, as relevant) gather useful information. Your last step is to interpret (analyze) the data in a timely manner to inform how you respond.

USE THE DATA TO INFORM HOW YOU TEACH

The data gathering approaches described in this chapter are used to help you screen for students in need of targeted support. Once you have identified this potential group of students, you will want to organize your data so that you can use it to make informed decisions. As a first step, the information should be graphed for analysis by you, the PBIS team, and/or other relevant teams, such as content or grade-level teams. For example, after the team has graphed the ODR data for each grade level in a PBIS school, students with the greatest number of ODRs at a chosen point in time would be given consideration to receive targeted supports. Cross-referencing the ODR data with attendance records may also suggest that particular students appear at risk with respect to missing school and declining grades. Once targeted supports are being delivered, you should continue to monitor these data sources regularly to ensure that the targeted supports are effective.

Matching Targeted Supports to Student Needs in PBIS Schools

After data are reviewed and students' needs are identified, students must receive quick access to supports. In PBIS schools, there may be a set timeframe for supports to be made available; in any case, this should occur in a timely manner, such as within 5 school days. How can arrangements be made this quickly? In Chapter 2, we recommended creating a list or resource map of the targeted supports that are already available in your school. In addition to listing the targeted supports available in your school, it is important to also note the entry criteria (who may qualify for this type of support), the data collection monitoring system (how will student progress be monitored), and the exit criteria (how to determine when students no longer need the targeted support). Compiling this information in one place simplifies and expedites the process of initiating supports for the students who need them. Table 3.3 provides an example of one such resource map.

When matching supports to students, consider the data that you have collected and analyzed to determine the students' needs, the resources available at your school, and the match between available supports and student needs. The type and intensity of support provided will vary based on student need. Some students may only require minor forms of support, such as small adjustments in school routines, whereas others may require more comprehensive forms of targeted support. For example, you may look at the data and decide to provide additional support to students who needed multiple reminders on expectations by having these students further define the expectations at an individual level and self-monitor their performance periodically during the day (e.g., times of day when they have historically demonstrated problem behavior). Support may be provided at a greater level to students who are identified as needing multiple reminders of expectations and who also have scores in the at-risk range on a given formal screener. In a PBIS school, this subset of students may be supported through a series of skills group sessions for a period of time (e.g., a social club that meets with guidance staff one time per week over 7 weeks) or through other more resource-intensive targeted supports. Continued assessment for the purposes of progress monitoring could logically involve collecting data on student performance in meeting expectations in combination with periodic use of the screener conducted

Table 3.3. Example of a Tier 2 intervention resource map for students identified as benefitting from targeted support

Resource/intervention	Description	Entry criteria	Data collected to monitor progress	Exit criteria
Group meetings with school counselor or psychologist	Students meet a minimum of one time per week (30 minutes) and up to three times per week to focus on student need, to talk about problems and solutions, to learn and practice coping strategies, and to monitor progress in using these skills.	A score in the at-risk range on a behavioral screener Repeated absences (more than four in any quarter or more); repeated missed work (more than two assignments from one teacher)	Data collected in group related to personal goals or goals of the group Weekly teacher report Weekly student self-report Weekly office discipline referral (ODR) data Weekly attendance data	Met criteria for personal or group goal. Report by teacher reflects consistent attendance and participatory behavior over a 3-week period.
Mentoring	Students meet a minimum of two times per week with a mentor to monitor weekly progress on preestablished goals.	A score in the at-risk range on a behavioral screener Repeated absences (more than four in any quarter or more); repeated missed work (more than two assignments from one teacher)	Data collected on personal goals by student and mentor Weekly ODR and attendance data	Met criteria for personal goal. Report by administrators reflects consistent attendance.

Social skills group	Students meet weekly with a counselor, psychologist, interventionist, or teacher for sessions that teach skills related to specific areas of concern for the group.	Obtained a score in the at-risk range on a behavioral screener Multiple ODRs over two quarters	Data collected on social skills components as introduced in the sessions Direct observation of social skills use in group and in generalized settings (classroom, cafeteria, playground) Direct observation of social skills use by teacher	Completion of a social skills component checklist with 90% accuracy across three sessions. Demonstrates use of skills across settings.
Check-In/Check-Out (Crone, Horner, & Hawken, 2004)	Students who are nominated as having continued behavioral challenges or have multiple ODRs in a marking period meet with the same staff member on frequent, scheduled intervals during the day.	Below basic scores or low academic achievement in any content area Below proficient performance on curriculum-based measures A behavioral screener score exceeding normative criteria for externalizing or internalizing behavior	Data collected daily on monitoring form to be signed by both the teacher and the parent	Met criteria of personal goals for consecutive weeks. Move into a maintenance phase involving self-monitoring and meet goals for consecutive weeks.

Source: Lane, Kalberg, and Menzies (2009).

> When a student receives a support, data analysis continues for the purposes of monitoring progress and determining if and when to fade use of the support.

earlier in the school year. The exit criteria for students in the targeted group may be that they are no longer being identified as being in the top three in your classroom for needing reminders on expectations and are also no longer scored at the at-risk level on the given screener.

In another example, suppose that you have a middle school student who has been nominated by multiple teachers for poor attendance (he was tardy or absent three times in the first quarter), not turning in work regularly, and three ODRs related to peer problems. Furthermore, on the behavioral screener being used, he scored in the at-risk range. The targeted supports listed on this school's PBIS resource map included a peer mentor program and homework club, along with potential access to social workers, mental health professionals, and counselors. The exit criteria for this student might include attending school on a consistent basis, turning in assignments, and consistently meeting classroom expectations as evidenced by being free of ODRs in the next marking period. With these goals in mind, the targeted support (Tier 2) team uses the resource map and considers which of the supports on the list would best meet the student's needs.

Matching Targeted Supports to Student Needs in Traditional Schools

The process of making an informed decision on what targeted interventions are needed to support a student is equally important in traditional school settings and should be done as quickly as possible. You have already started this process by creating your resource map of targeted support options that are available in your school. You are encouraged to consider this information as you answer the following questions:

1. At what level is the student performing now?

2. At what level do I want the student to be performing by the end of the marking period or year?

3. What types of support will more likely help the student to reach this goal?

The last question calls upon both your knowledge of the student and the information on your resource map at your school to select meaningful targeted supports. Addressing these questions can help you to match targeted supports to student needs. Although you may not have the benefit of a PBIS structure, you likely have some other team structure in place in your school that may help with developing and implementing support (e.g., individualized support teams [ISTs], student support teams [SSTs]). If not, there may be other people in your building to collaborate with who can add expertise and support you in providing targeted supports. For example, you may establish a small group of colleagues that could include your guidance counselor and other teachers.

A collaborative group can bring together the necessary resources for data collection and implementation, monitoring progress, and revising targeted supports over time. Share your resource map and plan with the group and revisit your answers to the previous questions. Customize this matrix for your student(s) by including the desired behavior, how often data will be collected and by whom, and what criteria will demonstrate that the student has achieved the goal.

Let's consider an example of how your (perhaps informal) team can work together to develop and implement targeted supports. Suppose you have a student, Natalie, who has difficulty coping with frustration. Some of the triggers that contribute to her "losing it" include when she has to engage in routines (e.g., get materials out, walk around the room, talk to others) prior to getting started on her work. Once started, Natalie does not like to stop working if her work is not completely finished; if you start to transition at that point, she will refuse to move to another activity. Her expression of this frustration can escalate to include throwing materials, trying to leave the room, and complaining loudly. You have tightened up your universal strategies, such as reviewing the schedule more often and giving her a transition reminder, which has helped some over the course of the past 3 weeks. Based on recording the amount of time Natalie takes to get started and switch, you have determined that she continues to miss at least 10 minutes of math instruction each day (Figure 3.1) and continues to engage in undesired behaviors that have you and the support staff concerned. She visits the office approximately two times a week. In addition, other teachers have reported similar patterns.

Based on the data presented and the knowledge of Natalie's interests and needs, your team decides that targeted support should include a study skills group that the guidance counselor runs. The counselor agrees to incorporate time management into the session to help Natalie with planning and carryover into the classroom. In addition, a self-monitoring checklist will be taught to give her a clear picture of how she is using her time in the classroom. The team will use the data from the self-monitoring checklist and ODR information to guide future decisions.

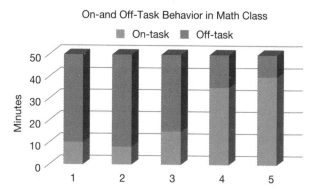

Figure 3.1.   Time on and off task for Natalie in math class for five observation periods (horizontal axis). Observations 4 and 5 show significant improvement following implementation of more frequent schedule reviews and transition reminders, but considerable off-task time persists.

Intensifying or Fading Supports

Student data need to be reviewed regularly to determine if sufficient progress is being realized. An effective data monitoring schedule allows for consistent review of data to ensure that a student does not go for an undue period of time without demonstrating progress. If a student is not making adequate progress, a timely decision as to what and how supports should be adjusted or intensified is required. If a student is making reasonable progress, supports can be continued or faded over time. When bringing data to team meetings, be sure to provide visual representations to facilitate analysis (e.g., graphs), gather feedback from each team member, and leave with a plan of action for each student.

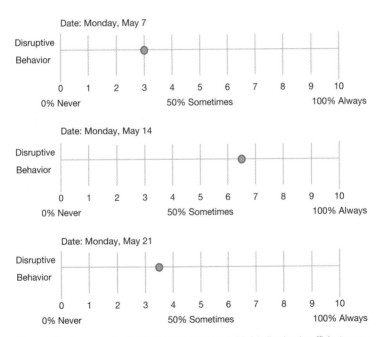

Figure 3.2. An example of direct behavior ratings (DBRs) indicating insufficient or no progress. It is estimated that on May 21 the student demonstrated disruptive behavior 35% of the class period.

Consider the scenario of a given student not demonstrating a sufficient response to targeted supports. This may be visually apparent through variability in the data (inconsistent performance), no progress over three or more data points, or a trend in the opposite direction than you desire (e.g., you want the behavior to decrease but it is increasing). A student who is not making sufficient progress or whose behaviors are getting worse may need more intensified supports. See Figures 3.2 and 3.3 and Table 3.4 for examples of trends regarding a student's progress in disruptive behavior and on-task behavior.

Students who do not show responsiveness to initially provided targeted supports may need more comprehensive targeted support. For example, Samuel has been reviewing expectations prior to each class period and using a self-monitoring checklist to determine if he is meeting the classroom expectations across the day. However, he has made little progress since starting this targeted approach a few weeks ago. First, look at the data to determine patterns in the behavior (e.g., what classes, what expectations). Second, talk with Samuel and other relevant staff involved with implementing targeted supports about the barriers to meeting the expectations. Third,

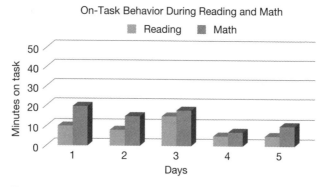

Figure 3.3. Additional example (graph) of tracking trends in a student's progress regarding disruptive behavior and on-task behavior during Reading and Math.

Table 3.4. Additional example (chart) of tracking trends in a student's progress regarding on-task behavior during Reading and Math

Date	Reading (total minutes = 50)	Math (total minutes = 50)
Day 1	10	20
Day 2	8	15
Day 3	15	18
Day 4	5	7
Day 5	5	10

talk with Samuel's parents about any changes at home or information that is being shared about school at home. Fourth, hone in on the most recent report card and CBA in the classes in which Samuel has the most trouble. For example, based on the previously noted considerations, you may find that Samuel feels that he is picked on or blamed for actions of others in his peer group. In addition, there may have been changes at home, such as no one being consistently available to check that Samuel is completing his work or keeping up with studying/homework due to a parent's work schedule. Based on this information, the team may decide that the student's needs align with additional targeted supports, such as the established mentor program in concert with the social skills group at this school.

CONCLUSION

A variety of data are critical for both screening and progress monitoring purposes when considering and implementing targeted supports. Depending on your school, different sources of data may be more readily available to you and/or your PBIS team. However, regardless of your specific resources, you will need to establish a method for identifying students to receive supports and monitoring their progress while the supports are being provided. In this chapter, we covered the basics of the kinds of data you might find most useful and what to do with that information.

Now that you have a basic understanding of how data can be used to inform your practice, the next couple of chapters help to further explain targeted supports in both a PBIS setting and a traditional school. Chapter 4 specifically addresses targeted supports in a PBIS school and provides guidance on how to integrate services and supports from other child-serving systems in your classroom. Chapter 5 provides you with guidance on what targeted supports look like in classrooms within a traditional school.

4

What Do Targeted Supports Look Like in a School Using PBIS?

T here is no single targeted support that is available in all schools implementing PBIS. However, there is a predictable menu of options that PBIS schools tend to gravitate toward as they install targeted supports. If you are working in a PBIS school, you should start by becoming familiar with the array of available targeted supports in your school building (i.e., create or obtain a resource map). It is not uncommon to find a few integrated types of targeted supports available. This is not to suggest that all PBIS schools will reflect a comprehensive array of integrated options. It is possible that your school may only operate one systematic approach to providing targeted supports. The key is for you to be aware of what is available and how to go about accessing these options. Table 4.1 highlights some of the more commonly available targeted supports in PBIS schools.

Table 4.1. Common targeted supports in schools implementing positive behavior interventions and supports (PBIS)

Name of targeted support	Brief overview
Check and Connect (Sinclair, Christenson, Evelo, & Hurley, 1998)	This support is designed for students with reoccurring behavior problems that are not considered dangerous. Check and Connect can be viewed as an example of a research-supported mentoring program. Emphasis is on improving students' positive relationships and prosocial behavior through positive interactions with school staff with increased frequency of reinforcement and feedback. The approach involves connecting the student with a school-based monitor to improve student engagement, improve attendance and punctuality, and prevent school dropout. The school monitor acts as a liaison between the student, school, family, and community. This person works individually with each assigned student to provide encouragement and to more closely monitor student success. There are typically two levels of delivery: basic (which usually involves monthly face-to-face student–monitor meetings) and intensive (which involves more frequent face-to-face student–monitor meetings).
Behavior Education Program (BEP; Crone, Horner & Hawken, 2004); also referred to as Check-In/Check-Out (CICO)	This support is designed for students with reoccurring behavioral problems that are not considered dangerous. Students carry with them a daily progress report (DPR) card to and from each class they go to during the day. The student and teacher(s) independently rate the student's performance during the class period at the end of each class period. Check-in and checkout meetings occur at predetermined times on a daily basis with the student's assigned staff member (typically not the classroom teacher, but it could be depending on how the school organizes this form of targeted support), with the assigned staff member providing feedback/encouragement to the student as well as documenting performance. Parents are encouraged to participate by signing off on DPRs when brought home by their child that same evening (and, in turn, the student brings the signed DPR back the next school day).

Name of targeted support	Brief overview
Check, Connect, and Expect (Cheyney, Lynass, Flower, Waugh, Iwaszuk, Mielenz, & Hawken, 2010)	This support is designed for students with reoccurring behavior problems that are not considered dangerous. The approach integrates component parts of Check and Connect and BEP (or CICO). School staff are positioned to establish an ongoing supportive relationship with targeted students (similar to Check and Connect), with a high frequency of interactions (typically daily) and feedback provided on behavioral performance through the use of a daily progress report (as in BEP/CICO). The use of student self-monitoring also is systematically built into this approach along with ongoing progress monitoring, leading to data-based decision making as to adjustments and/or exit from this targeted support.
Social skills instruction	This support is designed for students with reoccurring behavior problems that are not considered dangerous. Students meet as a small group on a regularly scheduled basis to receive additional instruction in targeted social skills that are of concern (e.g., anger management, conflict resolution, conversational skills). The lessons may be developed by school staff, use a selected curriculum, or reflect a combination of these two approaches. Two commonly employed established curricula include First Step to Success (Walker, Severson, Feil, Stiller, & Golly, 1998) and Second Step (Grossman, Neckerman, Koepsell, Liu, Asher, & Beland, 1997). For example, students might convene for a weekly 30-minute meeting in which they receive direct instruction, including participation in simulations regarding the use of targeted social skills. The instruction may be provided by a guidance counselor, designated teachers, or other staff, including paraeducators under the supervision of instructional staff. Periodic assessments, including simulated activities, occur in tandem with tracking behavioral performance data relevant to the students from outside of the sessions (in the typical ebb and flow of student performance across typical school days).

(continued)

Table 4.1. *(continued)*

Name of targeted support	Brief overview
Mentoring	This support is designed for students who are viewed as being at risk for developing antisocial behavior or unhealthy patterns of behavior, typically on the basis of screening indicators and/or past behavioral performance. As with curricular approaches to social skills instruction, there is an array of established mentoring programs (with varying degrees of supportive research), including Big Brothers Big Sisters and more locally designed mentoring programs. Mentoring involves pairing a targeted student with a mentor (who is typically an adult or older student) in the hope of developing a sustainable positive relationship. In many instances, the mentor is also intended to serve as a role model for the student (mentee). Also, in many instances there is little explicit connection with performance (behavioral) expectations, but this is not to suggest that such explicit connection could not be established by the mentor. Features of mentoring programs may vary; however, the most effective mentoring approaches reflect common elements such as 1) screening mentors and matching them to mentees, 2) training and support for mentors, 3) clear expectations for mentors in terms of meetings with the mentee and for such meetings (at least initially), and 4) documentation and reporting procedures.

Source: Hawken, Adolphson, MacKleod, and Shumann (2009).

TIER 2 SUPPORTS COMMONLY AVAILABLE IN PBIS SCHOOLS

The array of targeted supports at your disposal might be best illustrated through examples. To show more details of how each support works and how each can match certain student needs, this next section revisits the student examples we introduced in Chapter 1.

Check and Connect: How It Worked for Alexa

Alexa is a 13-year-old eighth grader who has performed reasonably well in most of her classes. However, she has become increasingly disruptive in math and science and also has been increasingly cutting these same classes. She struggles with problem-solving skills in tandem with a lack of sufficient coping skills for use in frustrating situations (e.g., during math and science). Alexa's middle school is entering its fourth year of implementing PBIS; this past year, it established a Check and Connect program. The Tier 2 team identified Alexa as a student who might positively respond to Check and Connect, based on her needs in the area of coping and problem-solving strategies.

Mrs. Smith is the school monitor for this targeted support program. She contacted Alexa's mother to describe the program and to address any questions that Alexa's mother might have before reaching out to Alexa. Mrs. Smith then arranged a first meeting with Alexa, with her mother's permission, to get to know Alexa a bit as well as to build a schedule of periodic meetings for the remainder of the marking period. One meeting per week was scheduled for the initial month of implementation. Over time, based on Alexa's progress, these meetings were tapered back gradually to once every 2–3 weeks. Emphasis during scheduled meetings was on providing additional levels of encouragement to Alexa regarding school performance as well as talking about matters of concern for Alexa, such as a few peer-related issues. Mrs. Smith also provided varying degrees of coaching Alexa on ways that she could more effectively communicate with her math and science teachers about frustrating issues. Both Alexa's math and science teachers also received encouragement and guidance to periodically review performance expectations with Alexa as well as to increase the frequency of providing praise statements to Alexa for class attendance and efforts. Mrs. Smith also stayed in contact with Alexa's mother and served as a primary point of contact.

Not surprisingly, it took a little bit of time for Alexa and her math and science teachers to notice significant change in her performance. However, after a couple of weeks, Alexa began to experience more positive days in math and science. Over time, Alexa developed additional coping skills as well as communication strategies (e.g., asking the math or science teacher for a quick break when she was frustrated). Learning these skills helped Alexa to gain confidence through positive experiences to the point that her involvement with the Check and Connect Program was able to be gradually faded over time.

Behavior Education Program (Check-In/Check-Out): How It Worked for Samuel

Samuel is a third grader who increasingly required redirection from his classroom teacher as well as the assigned adult volunteer in his classroom. He also increasingly pushed his classmates on the playground and threw temper tantrums when upset. Samuel's classroom teacher was in contact with both Samuel's mother and the building principal. Through those interactions, the Tier 2 team determined that Samuel might respond well to the school's Check-in/Check-Out (CICO) program. The elementary school was entering its third year of utilizing a PBIS framework, which included CICO as a targeted support program option.

Mr. Espinosa, the school's assistant principal, served as the primary progress monitor for students enrolled in the CICO program. Mr. Espinosa initially met with Samuel to describe how CICO worked and set the stage to start the process the next week. Samuel then started each day by checking in with Mr. E (as Samuel referred to him) to make sure he was ready for his school day. This check-in meeting included 1) collecting Samuel's DPR card—called a "thumbs-up card" at this school—that documented the previous day and was signed by his mother and 2) receiving a new card for the current day. Mr. E also provided encouragement for the day ahead.

Over the course of each day, Samuel's teachers provided feedback to him at the end of each class, electronically completed reports for all of his classes for the thumbs-up card, and submitted them to Mr. E before the end of the day. Samuel also carried his thumbs-up card with him throughout the day, self-evaluating his performance in terms of meeting expectations and then presenting it to Mr. E at the end of the day during their scheduled checkout meeting. During the check-out meeting, Mr. E would review Samuel's performance, as reported by teachers, by tallying points as well as by comparing Samuel's self-reported scores with his teachers' scores for that day. Mr. E provided Samuel with praise when Samuel achieved targeted goals for that day or guidance and encouragement for improving performance regarding instances when Samuel's performance did not meet expectations. Mr. E also provided Samuel with his scored thumbs-up card to carry home for his mother's signature and review. Mr. E maintained scheduled contact with Samuel's mother at the end of every 6-day cycle of instruction. In concert with the application of CICO, staff also provided some direct instruction in a few coping skills for Samuel (e.g., taking a deep breath, collecting his thoughts, and then determining a course of action when he felt upset; using cooperative play skills on the playground).

As a result of these targeted supports, Samuel experienced some relatively fast positive outcomes. Samuel continued in CICO for a little over 7 weeks, to the point where meeting behavioral expectations became the norm. Samuel's formal involvement in CICO was faded over time based on progress and performance.

Check, Connect, and Expect: How It Worked for Selina

Selina is a sixth-grade student who appeared to be painfully shy but had no history of acting in a manner that was considered disrespectful toward others. Although she had made reasonable academic progress in the past, her teachers expressed concern about her persistent withdrawn appearance and change in affect when working with other students, at times pulling away from others. Staff concern had particularly grown in association with Selina's complaints of stomach pain and nausea, resulting in frequent trips to see the school nurse. These concerns began with Selina's visiting the school nurse once or twice per week; however, this increased to the point of daily visits (and, on a few occasions, more than one trip to the nurse per day). Over the past few weeks, Selina and her parents visited various doctors, and Selina received a battery of medical examinations by specialists to explore the cause of her increasing degree of pain and nausea. Multiple tests yielded no diagnosis of a physical condition explaining Selina's increasing reports of discomfort. Staff members who had been present during Selina's reports of discomfort corroborated that Selina genuinely appeared to be in pain, to the degree that remaining in class would have made little sense during such episodes.

Selina's middle school was in its fourth year of implementing PBIS and provided an array of supportive approaches to their students. The Tier 2 team decided to have Selina try the school's Check, Connect, and Expect Program, combined with direct instruction in the use of calming skills for situations where she feels anxious in the classroom. This occurred in tandem with supporting Selina's parents to continue exploring physical and mental health assessments. Mrs. Tate, one of Selina's teachers with whom Selina appeared to feel most comfortable, agreed to serve as Selina's mentor teacher for the Check, Connect, and Expect program, and Selina appeared open to having her in this role.

At the start of each school day, about 10 minutes before homeroom period, Selina privately checked in with Mrs. Tate. Mrs. Tate provided some brief words of encouragement and overviewed the targeted goals on Selina's weekly goal card, which was organized to capture assessments of performance during class periods throughout the week. Selina's goals emphasized the use of calming skills to enable her to better cope with feelings of stress she might be experiencing. Selina carried her weekly goal card with her. Each teacher provided Selina with private encouragement throughout each class period for appropriate interaction with peers and completed an assessment of Selina's performance at the end of each class period. These assessments were also sent to Mrs. Tate. Selina presented her completed weekly goal card to Mrs. Tate at the end of each school day during a scheduled check-out session (which, like the check-in session, lasted 5–10 minutes). These check-out sessions emphasized reinforcement when Selina met her targeted goals on a given day and included encouragement and guidance as to how to meet expectations the next day. At the end of each week, Mrs. Tate reminded Selina about sharing her weekly goal card with her mother, who in turn signed off on the card; Selina then returned the card to Mrs. Tate at the first check-in session the following week.

In addition to these procedures, the school nurse proactively scheduled a few meetings with Selina to talk about triggers for Selina's episodes. Mrs. Tate instructed Selina on some general coping skills, along with preventive strategies emphasizing sleep, nutrition, and exercise. Although the process for obtaining further medical assessments (both physical and behavioral health) required additional time throughout the school year, the targeted supports helped Selina to function throughout each school day. Over the course of a few weeks, the frequency of episodes resulting in requests to leave class to see the nurse substantially decreased.

Social Skills Instruction: How It Worked for Tyler

Tyler, a young man in the eleventh grade, had an individualized education program (IEP) and was identified as having an emotional disturbance. Tyler received most of his instruction and special education services within general education classrooms. Tyler's high school had been implementing PBIS for 2 years and was just beginning to ramp up supports at advanced tiers. The increasing degree of problems experienced by Tyler in his PE class brought him to the attention of the Tier 2 team.

The primary concern included difficulties in following directions and acting in a safe manner. Specifically, Tyler was failing to follow rules during PE class to the point where he had been sent to the office on three separate occasions during the second marking period alone. Tyler generally got along reasonably well with peers at school. However, based on further exploration with Tyler and his teachers (particularly the PE teacher, Mr. Sneed), it became apparent that a major contributing factor influencing Tyler's behavior in PE class appeared to stem from subtle confrontations and disagreements that Tyler was having with a few classmates during competitive games. As a result, the Tier 2 team felt it would be appropriate to involve Tyler in a social skills training group that the high school recently initiated. This group was referred to as the Thursday Club because it convened on Thursdays during a common free period. Mr. Sneed initially contacted Tyler's parents, who were agreeable. The guidance counselor who coordinated the Thursday Club met with Tyler to explain the program. Tyler was scheduled to attend one of the two Thursday Club groups that had particular emphasis on resolving conflicts with others in a variety of situations. The guidance counselor, along with a team of three other teachers, provided direct instruction, including simulations with Tyler and the other students over the course of 8 weeks.

Because of Tyler's IEP, his involvement with the Thursday Club was implemented in a coordinated manner with his special education teacher, Ms. O'Brien. Ms. O'Brien also increased her frequency of contact with Mr. Sneed for a few weeks at the onset of initiating targeted supports to further ensure that all other relevant component parts of Tyler's IEP were being consistently delivered in PE class. The two teachers closely monitored Tyler's performance in PE throughout the entire time in which targeted supports were delivered. As Tyler further developed conflict resolution skills, his performance in PE class sufficiently improved over time. Tyler's direct involvement in the Thursday Club was tapered after 8 weeks. He could still attend Thursday Club meetings if he wished, but he was not required to do so as long as he continued to meet expectations across all of his courses, including PE.

Mentoring: How It Worked for Julie

Julie is a high-achieving tenth-grade student involved in a number of school activities. She has a history of success both in the classroom and socially with her classmates, and she is very popular with both staff and many students at her high school. Given this profile, at least on the surface, it appeared that there should be no concerns with Julie. However, she was increasingly feeling out of control, and her sleep patterns were becoming erratic. Julie reported this was in part due to overloading herself with so many things to do, as well as difficulties in managing the internal stress associated with her own expectations to excel in everything that she took on. She shared her feelings with one of her close friends, who in turn encouraged her to talk with a teacher. Julie's friend was persistent to the point that Julie did, in fact, talk with Mrs. Aurand, who was Julie's class advisor and her instructor in an advanced placement psychology course. Mrs. Aurand then consulted the guidance counselor and Tier 2 team.

Julie's high school had been implementing PBIS for the past few years and was in the process of trying to further refine its implementation to better integrate timely access to school- and community-based mental health services to students in need. The guidance counselor, Mrs. Aurand, Julie, and her parents sat down to talk through the concerns and to explore possible targeted supports for Julie. A number of targeted approaches were identified, with some starting immediately and others to be staggered in as soon as possible. The guidance counselor began to meet with Julie on a regular basis and, whenever Julie felt the need, was on call for her at school. Meetings were kept brief to avoid adding too much to Julie's schedule. Based on consensus of all involved, scheduled meetings occurred daily for a little more than a week while additional targeted supports were being organized.

The high school had been operating the Big Brothers Big Sisters Program as a part of providing additional targeted supports to students with particular profiles. Julie's profile did not appear to align with the design of that particular mentoring program; however, when talking with the guidance counselor, Julie had expressed interest in connecting with someone a little bit older than her who had previously had some similar experiences, preferably a young female professional or perhaps a college student. The Tier 2 team decided to establish an additional type of mentoring approach based on the current circumstances with Julie.

After considering a variety of options, the Tier 2 team reached out to a local university to recruit a small pool of high-achieving female students who might potentially become a mentor for Julie. Following the acquisition of required clearances and permission forms for all involved, the guidance counselor provided some initial training in mentoring to three potential mentors. Julie was provided opportunities to interact with all three students, and she felt particularly comfortable with one sophomore engineering major who herself had worked through some similar experiences in high school. Mentoring sessions were organized through the high school's guidance office and were scheduled to initially provide a high frequency of interactions (2–3 times per week), each short in duration (15–30 minutes per mentoring session). In the beginning of the mentoring relationship, all of the sessions occurred on high school grounds. Over time, based on opportunities and schedule constraints, mentoring sessions ebbed and flowed in terms of frequency, duration, and location.

The guidance counselor maintained close communication with Julie and her mentor. Documentation of mentoring sessions occurred on a regular basis. In tandem with implementing this approach to mentoring, guidance staff worked closely with Julie's parents to connect the family with agencies that participated in the family's insurance plan and could provide a mental health assessment. The assessment resulted in Julie's receiving community-based behavioral health treatment for an anxiety disorder. Although this array of targeted supports required some unique efforts, things came together reasonably well over the period of about 10 weeks. Julie realized great benefit from these coordinated targeted supports, and the school established an additional mentoring option for future use with other students.

COORDINATING SUPPORTS
FROM OTHER CHILD-SERVING SYSTEMS

Now that we have highlighted some of the more commonly available targeted supports in PBIS schools, let's turn our attention to talking a bit about how such targeted supports can help to meet the needs of students who may also be receiving treatment or supportive interventions from other child-serving systems, as was the case with Selina and Julie. It is not uncommon to have a portion of students who are in need of targeted or individual intensive supports at school also receive (or need to receive) supports from other provider agencies and systems, such as mental health, juvenile probation, or child protective services. The reason for delivery of those other services and supports, as well as the nature of those same services and supports, may vary from student to student. Many of the services and supports provided through these other systems are funded and oriented around providing medically prescribed or court-ordered services. Trying to navigate such interagency terrain may add to confusion for you as a teacher.

Our goal in the remainder of this chapter is to provide you with some practical guidance to better understand such situations and, in turn, be able to effectively communicate and collaborate with colleagues from other child-serving systems. Table 4.2 highlights the key aspects of interagency collaboration. The concepts and practices highlighted in this table should provide you with a firm foundation upon which to build effective collaboration with colleagues from other child-serving systems.

Moving beyond the basics noted in Table 4.2, let's consider a few scenarios that you may encounter as a classroom teacher. For example, Jean is a student who has been diagnosed

Table 4.2. Foundation for interagency collaboration when providing targeted supports at school

Foundation	Description
Understanding theoretical orientations and language among child-serving systems	Theoretical orientations (or paradigms) are somewhat like a pair of lenses that one might wear to be able to see more clearly. Not all sets of lenses are designed the same, just as you and your friend both may use eyeglasses but with different corrective lenses. As a teacher, you understandably view the world through an educational set of lenses, whereas mental health providers view that same world through a medical and/or therapeutic set of lenses. Others (e.g., a juvenile probation officer) will have yet another distinctive set of lenses (e.g., public safety, restorative justice). By acknowledging and respecting these different ways of seeing the world, you position yourself to be able to appreciate that different language sets also come with these different sets of lenses (e.g., terms such as *educational intervention plan* as compared with *mental health treatment plan*). Appreciating the presence of such differences can help you to become effective and increasingly efficient in communicating in a way that resonates with everyone involved in the collaborative process.
Authentic engagement of student and family voice	The phrase "nothing about us without us" should serve as a navigational mantra for interagency collaboration in your endeavors to provide targeted supports. You will need to determine, on a case-by-case basis, the best way to engage the student and his or her family in the collaborative decision-making process. This will require use of common, jargon-free language in tandem with supporting the student and family to express what they view as desired outcomes. Meaningfully including student and family perspectives when providing targeted supports can enhance effectiveness and time efficiency for everyone.
Securing release of information to be able to communicate among relevant child-serving agencies	Information concerning any given student in your classroom is considered private (confidential). This is also the case for a mental health worker who provides treatment to a student and his or her family and for an assigned juvenile probation officer. Given the private nature of such information, and the value in being able to pull together various sources of information

Foundation	Description
	to provide targeted supports, obtaining permission (from the parent/legal guardian and/or student, depending on his or her age) is required to be able to appropriately share information with those representing other child-serving systems. Your school should have an established release of information form (or forms) to use for obtaining such approval. Each of the other child-serving agencies should also have such a form to use for obtaining permission to release information. Obtaining informed consent is essential to the interagency collaborative process.
Establishing a clear protocol for interagency collaboration	Establishing agreed-on procedures concerning how communication is to occur between you and others (and among the group in general) can enhance collaborative decision making. As a teacher, you will want to clarify with your immediate supervisor (e.g., building principal) your school's expectations in terms of communication and, in turn, use this as a frame of reference for determining agreed-on communication procedures with colleagues from other child-serving systems. Communication may occur in many forms, including verbal statements, formal and informal written correspondence, and interpersonal dynamics during face-to-face meetings (e.g., body language, tone of voice, active listening). Remember that the previously noted differences in theoretical orientations and language will translate into practice and thus should be incorporated within the protocol that you establish with colleagues from other child-serving systems.
Articulating shared goals and objectives among staff from various child-serving systems	As you communicate using the established protocol, you will want to reach agreement on common goals and objectives, which should provide a clear focus on organization of the targeted supports to be provided. By doing this, you increase the likelihood of coordinated services, if not one integrated approach to providing targeted supports (thus minimizing the likelihood of fragmented and disjointed approaches). It is not uncommon for a student receiving supports at advanced tiers to be involved with one or more other child-serving systems. Establishing agreed-on common goals and objectives helps to ensure that everyone's time and energy are well invested.

(continued)

Table 4.2.   *(continued)*

Foundation	Description
Clarifying roles and functions of staff among systems to achieve agreed-on goals and objectives	Once agreed-on goals and objectives are established, you will want to turn attention to defining what needs to be provided, by when, and by whom. There should be a focus on how the agreed-on supports from other child-serving systems will be implemented within your classroom (as relevant), too. The more precise and detailed this discussion, the better—this will help minimize confusion during implementation of targeted supports at school and specifically within your classroom. Depending on the nature and location of the services to be provided by staff from other child-serving systems, this may also require establishment of an interagency agreement (in writing) clearly describing who has supervisory authority of staff from those other child-serving systems while on school grounds. This type of interagency agreement helps to increase clarity of targeted supports for the student(s) of concern and minimizes the chance of you as the classroom teacher being placed in an awkward situation.
Providing clear and timely communication	One of the most precious resources that you have as a teacher is your time. This is also the case for your students because there is no such thing as a do-over from the previous day in that student's life. Targeted supports need to be easily accessible within a timely manner (typically within 3–5 school days). Providing detail and clear communication among relevant parties facilitates timely student access to effective targeted supports. Both individual communications and notes from any interagency team meetings should be clearly written and disseminated in a timely manner.
Resource sharing and braiding	Your time and knowledge about classroom operations and student performance are likely the most immediate resources that you will be sharing with colleagues from other child-serving systems (based on approval to release information, of course). However, depending on the degree of need with your student(s) receiving targeted supports, there may be need to further look to "braid" resources from your school and other systems to provide necessary targeted supports. Such intertwining of resources will likely require administrative approval from your

Foundation	Description
	school as well as the other funding system. For example, in one PBIS school, county prevention dollars from child protective services were used to partially underwrite aspects of operating Check and Connect as a targeted support. Be sure to keep your building administrator (e.g., principal) in the loop of communications concerning resources.
Ongoing progress monitoring and joint problem solving to achieve agreed-on goals and objectives	In light of the agreed-on shared goals and objectives, how your student(s) of concern responds to the targeted supports should be tracked. In turn, these data should be shared within the established team meeting protocol. Understandably, you will gather progress monitoring data respective to both academic and behavioral performance while your counterparts from other child-serving systems will likely have their own parallel forms of data they will concurrently gather as established by requirements of their respective systems. Given that approval for release of information has been obtained by your school and the other relevant child-serving agencies, the sharing of this information can help to inform decision making among all relevant parties.

with an anxiety disorder through the local mental health system and subsequently receives services and supports through a local mental health provider. One component of these services comes in the form of a therapeutic resource specialist (TRS), who accompanies Jean for a portion of the school day in your classroom. This TRS has a prescribed treatment plan that is to be implemented with Jean to (ideally) prevent problems from arising as well as to de-escalate the situation when problems do arise.

However, you also have your own approach to both prevention and early intervention in place within your classroom management system, and your classroom system is nested within your school's approach to implementation of PBIS. Do *not* presume that both approaches (PBIS at school and in your classroom and the treatment plan to be carried out by the TRS) will magically align and smoothly integrate with one another. Intuitively, you might hope for this to happen; however, our experiences suggest that this rarely happens on its own. Furthermore, the worst time for you to realize that the approaches are disjointed is when you are in the midst of trying to de-escalate a crisis with Jean.

Therefore, rather than waiting for this situation to arise, we encourage you to proactively talk through your approach to universal prevention and targeted supports at school with the TRS (perhaps including both your building administrator and the TRS's supervisor). When having this proactive conversation, start by identifying the obvious areas of common ground—Jean and her growth and development. Talk through your classroom management approach within your PBIS framework at school and, in turn, have the TRS talk through the treatment plan. Try to use conversational language as opposed to using acronyms or other forms of professional jargon. Use examples to illustrate or make things visible and tangible, and then agree upon general operating procedures for how the TRS will implement the treatment plan in the context of the operation of your classroom management system. Many situations that can become problematic in classrooms associated with coordinated efforts, as depicted in this scenario, can be avoided by having such a proactive meeting. This is not to suggest that issues will never arise, but we do believe that taking this course of action will minimize the chance of what should be nonissues becoming problematic issues in your classroom.

> Regular communication and proactive meetings to plan the day-to-day logistics of interagency collaboration can keep confusion and problems to a minimum.

An additional aspect of interagency approaches that can become somewhat tricky to navigate is a child's treatment plan being implemented at school in the presence of other students in your classroom. This is something to be considered and addressed through planning. In particular, there will likely be a close correlation between the degree of comfort felt by both you and the other agency provider (e.g., TRS) and the comfort of all of the students in your classroom. The more you can incorporate the TRS within the typical ebb and flow of daily operations in the classroom, the more likely it is that everyone will view this interagency approach as the norm. This can be initially planned through an organizing meeting as previously described. Alternatively, if time does not permit during the meeting, planning can occur through virtual communications (e.g., e-mail conversations) following your initial meeting. Either way, clearer communication between the adults on expectations and roles in the classroom will result in more comfortable—and ultimately effective—services and supports for everyone.

Another aspect of interagency endeavors that can lead to confusion is that different child-serving systems (e.g., schools vs. mental health agencies) have different eligibility criteria and subsequent arrays of services and supports. To be clear, it is *not* the job of the classroom teacher to become completely fluent in the language and culture of all other relevant child-serving systems. However, being aware that such differences exist is important to position yourself to effectively communicate with all relevant parties (including the student and parents).

As you know, education is an entitlement for all children in the United States, and students receiving special education services are specifically entitled to a free appropriate public education in the least restrictive environment (IDEA 2004). Although there are certain societal and legal requirements associated with other child-serving systems, many times the services provided by other child-serving systems are voluntary (short of a court order) and may be challenging to access in a timely manner (e.g., a child who is referred to receive counseling may face delays in finding a provider to deliver those counseling services). When health insurance is involved, variations in coverage can make things even more complex. It is important to understand that such differences in eligibility and service delivery systems exist and to proactively (before a problem arises) establish clear lines of communication to talk through such issues should they arise. Again, proactively anticipating such challenges and establishing communication should help to minimize a common problem that can emerge when delays or changes in services and supports are experienced: a breakdown in trust among the collaborating partners (you, the TRS or other service provider, the student, and the family). More transparent and easily tracked communications can decrease the likelihood of problems moving forward; if problems do surface, those problems may be more amicably resolved in a timely manner. Again, these types of communication structures do not typically just emerge by themselves. Rather, they require proactive planning.

Yet another area of possible confusion that may emerge as you increasingly work with other child-serving agencies has to do with aligning those other agency endeavors with an IEP if a student is receiving special education services. Regardless of whether you are a new or experienced teacher, navigating the special education process can sometimes feel overwhelming. This can feel even more complicated when aligning services and supports from other child-serving agencies in context of design and delivery of a student's IEP.

Although the number of potential issues that may arise for you are too many in number and too diverse in nature to adequately address in this book, one of the more common questions is about what gets written into the IEP. You may wonder how should it be written and where should it be placed within the document. First and foremost—and particularly important to you if you are not a special education teacher—is to make sure that someone with special education expertise is a part of the collaborative process. Furthermore, when organizing targeted supports involving other agencies for a student within an IEP, planning and decision making should occur within the established IEP team planning process. If the consensus of the IEP team is that the student of concern needs a particular service in order to benefit from special education (e.g., formal counseling to address concerns with anger management and related development of coping skills), that service should be noted in the child's IEP. The decision-making process on what is built into the IEP is an IEP team decision—not the decision of any other team or one person, regardless of title or expertise. However, it is relevant to also remember that whatever gets written into an IEP has resource implications for your school system (e.g., access to formal counseling on a weekly basis, as previously noted as an example). We do not share this fact as a disincentive for your collaboration within an IEP team leading to noting any given service within the IEP. Rather, you should ensure that your efforts to organize targeted supports involving other agencies for a student within an IEP are aligned within the context of IEP team operations (as relevant). In addition, a school administrator with decision-making authority concerning resources should be a part of the IEP team decision-making process.

> When targeted supports for a student with an IEP are being delivered through other agencies, arrangements must be made in collaboration with the student's IEP team.

On a final note, with the understanding that it is not possible to project the entire universe of situations you may encounter through your interagency experiences, we would be remiss if we failed to note the importance of clearly aligning your interagency efforts within the established protocol that your school employs with respect to implementation of the PBIS framework. For example, your PBIS school may be on the threshold of just beginning to formally incorporate local mental health staff members and school resource officers in promotion activities associated with your Tier 1 (universal level) team. Alternatively, perhaps your school has been implementing PBIS for a few years and has evolved in practice to the point where local mental health staff and your school resource officer are already situated on your school's Tier 1 team. Regardless of the degree of sophistication of implementation of PBIS in your school, it is important to have a clear understanding of the current degree of interagency presence and processes within your school's PBIS operations and to situate your efforts within this larger context. Such an understanding may be written into what is referred to as a Memorandum of Agreement (MOA) between your school and other child-serving agencies. However, it is also important to operationally define the MOA through proactive conversations, as previously described. This can be particularly critical in the event that a student does not sufficiently respond to targeted supports (including coordination of services and supports from other child-serving systems) and may therefore be in need of individualized intensive (Tier 3) supports at school.

CONCLUSION

Schools implementing PBIS already have structures in place for the many tasks involved in providing targeted supports (albeit to varying degrees). You likely have schoolwide procedures for identifying students who may benefit from targeted supports, a menu of support options, and procedures for monitoring progress and ultimately fading out supports. Navigating these protocols and options can be challenging, especially in cases where you are collaborating with other child-serving agencies, but the PBIS team is there to help. In Chapter 5, we discuss strategies that teachers can use if their schools are not (as of yet) implementing PBIS. As noted before, targeted supports can still be undertaken in a given classroom and can still be vitally useful.

5

What Do Targeted Supports Look Like in a Classroom in a Traditional School?

E ven among PBIS schools, there is not a single targeted support that is consistently available in every school. Furthermore, among schools not implementing PBIS, there is likely considerable variation in resources available. As a teacher in a traditional school, you may be more on your own to organize or develop supports. In this chapter, we discuss what that process looks like and what supports can entail, using a student example to illustrate possibilities.

FIRST STEPS IN PLANNING TARGETED SUPPORTS

Once you are aware which of your students are in need of Tier 2 support, you should provide these resources to your student(s) as quickly as possible. The data that you have already collected (as described in Chapter 3) will help you to determine the following:

1. What student behaviors do you wish to increase?

2. What student behaviors do you wish to decrease?

3. What is the goal, or how are these behavior changes meaningful with respect to student needs?

Setting Support Goals for Tyler

In Chapter 1, we introduced Tyler, who was having trouble in PE class with respect to following directions and being safe. We revisited his example in Chapter 4, looking at how Tyler could be served by targeted supports in a PBIS school. Here, we instead think about targeted supports for Tyler in a more traditional school setting. We review how data can be used strategically to establish a goal and to select a targeted intervention; then, we look at how to implement the intervention strategy in the classroom.

It was obvious to the staff members that Tyler was having problems. Use of their data helped to pinpoint patterns. Tyler was being sent to the office weekly for unsafe behaviors (e.g., confrontations and disagreements with peers, refusal to participate) and had accumulated a number of ODRs in the past month. In talking with Tyler, it became apparent that he did not agree with the rules that the teacher established for games or how the other students played according to those rules. The teacher thought about the behaviors to increase with Tyler: time spent in gym class, appropriate participation in activities, and adherence to the rules of the game. The teacher also thought about the behaviors of concern to decrease: behaviors that violate rules, yelling, and leaving the area without permission. Next, the teacher developed the goal: Tyler will attend and successfully participate in PE during games with other students throughout the marking period.

SELECTING TARGETED SUPPORT OPTIONS

Once a goal has been established, the next step is identifying the type of targeted support that will help the student to achieve the goal. A few data-based decision-making questions to help guide your selection of targeted support are outlined in Figure 5.1. Let's look at Tyler's needs:

1. Does Tyler need to further develop skills? Need support to use skills? Require attention? Need a combination of skill development, expanded support, and increased attention and support?

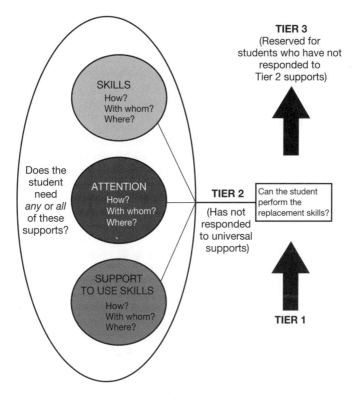

Figure 5.1.   Data-based decision questions, based on the function-based intervention decision model. (*Source*: Umbreit, Ferro, Liaupsin, & Lane, 2007.)

2. Who could provide the needed instruction, attention, and supports?

3. Is an adult or a peer a better match to provide skills/supports to Tyler?

4. Are there people that Tyler naturally connects with already available?

5. Can Tyler identify the behavior of concern?

Remember, providing targeted supports is a problem-solving process. Therefore, you are trying to reach the best solution with the information you have at your disposal.

Based on the information presented and the goal of full participation for Tyler, now think about your targeted support options. Think back to Chapter 2 and your targeted support resource map. Think about your established preliminary list of the Tier 2 resources available. Ask yourself, "What intervention might link well to the skills and/or support needed to reach Tyler's goal?" Use your answers to the previously noted data-based decision-making questions to determine if you will need to teach a new skill or reinforce an existing skill as part of your intervention. Table 5.1 provides you with some guidance to align targeted supports based on student needs. Viewing the established goals in this way should help you think about targeted intervention more clearly.

To be most efficient, you are encouraged to build relationships with colleagues at your school (e.g., teachers, guidance counselor, administrators) who can help to support your classroom endeavors. In Tyler's example, communication between the PE teacher and colleagues implementing the supports throughout this process is important. Keep in mind that you are layering these targeted supports on top of universal prevention strategies. Along these same lines, one goal is to see if you can increase promotion of prevention strategies being used by other colleagues. In Tyler's example, you could encourage the use of a simple precorrection strategy, such as a reminder of the expectation at the beginning of class. This may be as simple

Table 5.1. Aligning targeted supports based on student needs

Teaching new skills to address student needs	Potentially appropriate targeted supports to increase fluency
Additional instruction in specific skills or additional time dedicated to completing work	Study skills training or homework clubs
Social skills to foster better relationships with peers	Social skills groups; peer-mediated supports
Reminders and motivators for improving attendance and on-task behavior	Self-monitoring and/or mentoring
Reminders for staying on task and following regular behavior expectations	Enhanced classwide group contingencies; behavior contracting
Guidance from a role model or confidant with personal experience in a given situation	Mentoring

This table shows general areas that supports can address, but this is not a prescription. Selecting supports for your specific students should be based on each individual student situation and what is available at your school.

as providing a review of the expectations (universal prevention strategy), which will also set the stage for the generalization and maintenance of the desired behavior over time. For example, you may notice that Tyler gets upset at the beginning of games when the teams are picked. Perhaps the teacher could work with all of the students to gain an understanding of the importance of considering others' feelings in terms of being included, potentially also rethinking how teams are assigned. Furthermore, the conflict resolution strategies that Tyler is acquiring could be further reinforced by the PE teacher.

Another opportunity for support in your building may be in the form of talking with your school's guidance counselor. For example, there may already be some social skills groups that he or she could help you tap into for Tyler. You likely included these programs in your resource mapping. You are also encouraged to add programs to your resource map as new programs emerge in your school.

In Tyler's case, it may be possible to work with a number of different types of targeted supports to increase class participation. For example, skills training often is combined with self-monitoring or is used in tandem with enhanced classwide contingencies to reinforce desired behavior. In other words, targeted supports such as these (as well as others) can be aligned and concurrently provided (packaged together). We encourage you to consider the following targeted support options in your classroom based on your student needs. Each of these options is described for Tyler to illustrate their use.

Social Skills Training

Tyler needs to develop skills in understanding how game rules work in PE and how to work in a group (including ways to amicably resolve conflicts) as well as coping skills. You can provide Tyler with lessons to build these prosocial behaviors from social skills curricula (see Table 5.2 for a list of social skills training resources) or you can develop your own lessons based on your knowledge of the student and the situation.

There are two important things to keep in mind when developing social skills training in your classroom. First, students need regular and consistent training times. It is not about having one supersized lesson. Rather, the number of sessions and amount of time per session are dependent on the targeted skills and the student. When students are first learning a skill, they need to be provided with repetition. Maybe you could have Tyler, along with a small group of other students who also need to further develop conflict resolution skills, meet every day or every other day for 10- to 15-minute sessions. Alternatively, you may find an opportunity to do a 20- to 30-minute session over lunch once a week, then reinforce the skill in two smaller 10-minute sessions during that week. Make sure

> For effective social skills training, make sure instructional sessions are regularly scheduled, but also remember the quality of each session is more important than filling a set length of time.

Table 5.2. Social skills training resources

Resource	Reference
The ACCESS Program	Walker et al. (1988)
The Hidden Curriculum for Understanding Unstated Rules in Social Situations	Myles, Trautma, and Schelvan (2013)
I Can Problem Solve: An Interpersonal Cognitive Problem Solving Program	Sure (2001)
Peacemakers Program	Shapiro et al. (2002)
Second Step	Frey et al. (2005)
Skillstreaming the Adolescent	McGinnis (2011a)
Skillstreaming in Early Childhood	McGinnis (2011b)
Skillstreaming the Elementary School Child	McGinnis (2011c)
Social Skill Intervention Guide: Practical Strategies for Social Skills Training	Elliot and Gresham (1991)
Stop & Think Social Skills Program	Knoff (1990)
Teaching Social Skills to Youth	Dowd and Tierney (1995)
Think Social!	Winner (2006)

you create a schedule that is realistic for you to implement on a consistent basis. Second, the length of the session is not as important as the quality of the session. Use direct instructional strategies to provide opportunities to initially teach the skill and reinforce the skills through practice. We encourage you to use simulations or role playing when instructing social skills with your students.

In Tyler's case, you need to teach strategies that he can use when he gets upset so he can appropriately communicate his frustration to others. One way to approach this is to use real examples and establish a social skills group that teaches coping skills, such as requesting to take a break, cooling down, and returning/re-entering a situation. Be sure to give examples of strategies for conflict resolution and instruct through simulation. You may vary the simulated games you play with your students. In Tyler's case, you might also teach changes in the rules that may come up in PE class, issues that may come up with other students, or variations of games to help Tyler generalize the skills to other settings and situations. Remember that practicing the skill and specifically praising Tyler for desired behavior will help acquisition and generalization of the skills.

Self-Monitoring

A second option is to help Tyler learn to self-monitor his own behavioral performance (e.g., use of a conflict resolution strategy, asking for a break, following directions). Self-monitoring involves selecting the skill to target, setting a goal for the targeted skill, developing a way to have the student self-prompt the use of his or her strategy, checking progress on a regular schedule, graphing performance data, reviewing the data with the student, and rewarding goal achievement. The Direct Behavior Rating (DBR) method may be a good place to start for self-monitoring. The DBR could be incorporated into a student's daily routine to increase appropriate behavior over a period of time. Self-monitoring can help a student such as Tyler in performing the desired skill with minimal external prompting from you or other teachers. You could also independently rate behavioral performance and then compare your scores with Tyler's scores. Conducting a comparison session provides you with an opportunity to explain the similarities and differences in the scores and provide reinforcement and further guidance. It also provides time for Tyler to reflect on why there may have been differences in scores and to look at the data to see progress or where he needs to improve.

There are additional tools that can also help students such as Tyler with self-management. For example, you could use a timer that vibrates

> Student self-monitoring of behavior performance reduces reliance on other staff for prompting and feedback.

(e.g., MotivAider) at a preset time interval to cue him to self-monitor. This can help him to build increasingly independent use of self-monitoring strategies, assess the learning of skills, and reduce reliance on you or other staff.

Enhanced Classwide Group Contingencies

Using enhanced classwide group contingencies is an additional reinforcement strategy that relies on peers in the group to promote changes in the behavior of peers. Simple group contingencies are often used as a universal prevention (Tier 1) approach in classrooms. Emphasis through universal prevention is placed on review of expectations, and groups within your classroom are reinforced for meeting those expectations. A variation (enhancement) of this universal approach can be applied to provide targeted (Tier 2) support, targeting a skill that a small group of students are struggling to obtain (e.g., conflict resolution in Tyler's case). In addition to small group instruction, this skill is reviewed with the whole class, students model the targeted behavior, and examples and nonexamples are provided (much like the process when you provided initial instruction on your classroom expectations earlier in the year). Groups are then reinforced on a schedule when all members of their group apply the targeted skill to the situation at hand. Rewards are earned for reaching a specific criteria.

> Enhanced classwide group contingencies allow you to tap into other students' motivation and the power of positive peer pressure.

To illustrate enhanced classwide group contingencies through a different example from Tyler, suppose that you are teaching a fifth grader named Kevin who is struggling with talking during class. He often speaks when others, including you, are speaking. He often interrupts you during instruction and raises his voice above an appropriate level. Kevin is receiving an average of five reminders per day to lower his voice and to raise his hand when he has a question during instruction.

Some strategies you could use with Kevin include providing visual cards with pictures to represent a quiet voice and raise one's hand. You could set aside 5 minutes at the beginning and middle of the day to teach and review these skills with Kevin. As a part of scaffolding success for Kevin once he has acquired these skills over time, you could gradually delay calling on him until two others have talked, as long as he is sitting quietly. Furthermore, you could plan to increase this criteria over time based on progress with Kevin. As you apply this approach, you should also show Kevin's group ways to gently remind him by using a visual cue, such as holding up an index finger to represent *wait* and a pat on the back to show that they support him. You could also place paper clips in the group's reinforcement jar for every 10 minutes of the 50-minute class period that the students in the group (including Kevin) quietly participate, providing the group with a total of five opportunities to earn the group reinforcement. An additional variation of this technique involves what is referred to as *response cost*. To illustrate response cost, you would award five paper clips per period at the start of class, with one being removed for each 10-minute interval that the group did not meet the expectation. Students typically respond better to earning than taking away.

Facilitating a Mentor Relationship

Mentoring may be provided in a variety of ways and for a variety of purposes. The mentor may be a peer, an older student, or an adult. Across all forms, however, the primary focus of mentoring is fostering a positive relationship between the mentor and mentee. The relationship is what enables mentors to offer meaningful influence.

Well-developed peer mentoring programs provide explicit guidance on behavioral expectations for how mentoring occurs for both the mentor and mentee. For example, a peer mentor can be supportive and understanding, as well as help the mentee to set an action plan with a timeline toward achievement of a targeted goal. This requires a certain amount of skill that you may need to teach to the peer who is to serve as a mentor. Students can learn to be effective peer mentors with pre-established expectations and some training. Peer mentoring works for many students, although it will require time because you will need to foster this relationship to ensure success.

You might also consider an adult rather than peer mentoring relationship. This could involve working with people from your community that come into your classroom. For example, you may have access to a young professional in your town who could be recruited to connect with a given student. In other instances, it may be that another school staff member or you personally prove to be the best match for the student of concern. However, serving as an adult mentor for one of your own students should probably be your last option.

Mentoring programs can look different depending on student needs and the support structures available in your school community. Mentoring provides added support and structured opportunities to provide increasingly constructive interactions with targeted students. Mentoring sessions, on occasion, may be more related to simply spending time talking through issues that are causing problems and collaboratively establishing realistic goals to continue to review towards completion. On other occasions, mentoring can parallel the CICO procedure (albeit meeting on a much less frequent basis), where a checklist is used to monitor grades, responsibilities, and follow-through in the form of what was referred to in Chapter 2 as Behavior Progress Reports (BPRs). Many people often participate in the BPR process because other teachers and parents give feedback and sign the student's card. The student interactions in this case with the mentor are brief,

Table 5.3. General guide to establishing a mentoring program

Step	Recommendations
Recruit mentors	Ideally, the mentee should have voice in the decision-making process. Possible sources include peers, students from upper grades or local colleges, professionals in the local county, staff at school, or local retirees.
Establish mentor expectations	Be clear about expectations, including time commitment, portraying optimism and honesty, providing supportive acceptance in a nonjudgmental manner, and serving as a role model.
Establish mentee expectations	Be clear about expectations, including time commitment, communicating in an open/honest manner, and clarity about the role of the mentor.
Provide training and support to mentors	Provide instruction, as needed, in rapport building, positive reinforcement, goal setting, and action planning. In addition, provide clear protocol as to issues of confidentiality and issues that must be reported.

serving to review the BPR card and provide reinforcement. Additional sessions can also be added to work on social problem solving when warranted.

Many secondary schools have existing peer mentoring programs (e.g., Big Brothers Big Sisters). However, if no mentoring program exists, you are encouraged to consider starting such targeted support. The key to creating a meaningful mentoring program, should you need to establish one, is ensuring consistency in implementation to achieve your goal with the student. Some general guidelines to establishing a mentoring program are provided in Table 5.3.

Behavior Contracting

As touched on in Chapter 2, behavior contracts are systematic, student-centered ways of defining behavioral expectations in more detail; they are designed to increase reinforcement of a student for correct behavior. As with many targeted supports, behavior contracts should be considered a temporary measure, and there should be set goals for improvement over a reasonable amount of time. The key steps in establishing a behavior contract are as follows:

1. Create clearer operational definitions of the behavior expectations of concern.

2. Set goals for improvement.

3. Set a schedule for measuring performance and providing reinforcement.

You also need to identify reinforcers that you believe the student will find of value to use contingently based on performance.

Perhaps the trickiest part of designing an effective behavior contract is determining how frequently to evaluate and measure student performance. You will need to first think about the current frequency of the student's problem behavior (e.g., the student of concern engages in problem behavior requiring redirection on average one time per class period or perhaps one time each morning and one time each afternoon). Once you have identified the baseline frequency of the problem behavior, you will next need to use this information in tandem with your goal of achieving the 4:1 ratio of positive reinforcement for appropriate behavior as compared with redirection for problem behavior to establish a reasonable time interval for evaluation and measurement.

To illustrate, say that Jamal, a first-grade student, is engaging in significant problem behavior to the point that you must stop instruction and redirect the student on average one time per morning and one time per afternoon. Given this baseline, you would need to measure behavioral performance minimally five times each morning and five times each afternoon in order to achieve the 4:1 ratio. In another example, a seventh-grade student, Carl, engages in problem behavior, on average, one time every class period. In Carl's case, you would likely need to break the class period down into five intervals to measure five times per class period to achieve the 4:1 ratio. These two general examples, albeit relatively simplistic, are provided to help you understand how to go about targeting a reasonable time interval for measurement. Of these two examples, the latter illustration would likely be more challenging to you as a classroom teacher because it requires shorter time intervals, resulting in more frequent measurement.

Beyond the basics of contracting described previously, you will also want to think about building in a bonus clause, which may further incentivize your student and also provide you with a threshold as to when you will look to renegotiate the contract. As stated earlier, the primary goal is for you as the teacher to see sufficient improvement in behavior so that you can wean the student off the contract within a reasonable amount of time. This may require a couple of cycles of increasing criterion for performance over time based on student progress. Figures 5.2 and 5.3 provide examples of behavior contracts for Jamal and Carl. Note that all relevant staff are listed on the contract, as are the specifics about the target behavior, data collection procedures, methods for reinforcement, and potential consequences if the target criterion for performance is not achieved.

Continuing with the story of Jamal, at first you would evaluate and measure behavioral performance five times each morning and five times each afternoon, for a total of ten measures per day. Let's say that you established the initial target criterion for Jamal to earn eight out of ten smiley faces on his behavior chart card each day; at the end of the day, he can use those points toward an established pool of reinforcers. Given this scenario, perhaps you established the bonus clause as 5 consecutive days of meeting the criterion (eight out of ten smiley faces), which results in Jamal earning a special reward in addition to the daily reinforcers he has been earning. Furthermore, extending this line of thought, you also target the earning of two consecutive bonus payoffs as the threshold, at which time you will renegotiate the contract. Therefore, this means that once Jamal achieves eight out of ten smiley faces for 5 days in a row, he gets a special reward; once he consecutively earns two of these bonus rewards (10 consecutive days),

Behavior Contract

Student: Jamal Hall   Today's date: 2/8/16

Student's grade/teacher: First grade / Jill Blaine

Relevant staff: Jill Blaine and Corey Smith (paraeducator)

Target behavior (behavioral expectation):

Be responsible: Focus on your work.
                   Follow directions the first time.
                   Organize and get to work promptly.
                   Make a good effort.

Data collection procedure:
Use a Good Behavior Chart to evaluate Jamal's behavior five times each morning and five times each afternoon during the school day, using a smiley face for appropriate behavior and a sad face for inappropriate behavior. Staff and Jamal independently evaluate Jamal's behavior five times each morning and afternoon.

Reinforcement procedure (what and how often):
Jamal can randomly choose from the Gold Jar at the end of each day when he has earned 8 of 10 smiley faces on his behavior chart. The Gold Jar contains low-cost items of interest to Jamal, such as having an extra turn as line leader when going to the cafeteria or receiving a high-five from the school principal.

What must the student do to earn reinforcement?

Be responsible: Focus on your work.
                   Follow directions the first time.
                   Organize and get to work promptly.
                   Make a good effort.

Criterion: 8 of 10 smiley faces earned each day.

Consequences for failure to meet behavioral expectations:
Jamal will not earn access to the Gold Jar. Other relevant consequences may be implemented as deemed appropriate or necessary by Jamal's teacher(s).

Bonus for exceptional behavioral performance:
When Jamal meets expectations 5 consecutive days in a row, he may make a random choice from the Pot of Gold, a bucket decorated like a pot of gold and containing coupons for free movie passes and other items of value to Jamal. When Jamal earns two consecutive bonus picks (10 days in a row at 8 of 10 smiley faces), we will renegotiate the contract.

Signatures of all stakeholders:

_____

_____

_____

_____

Figure 5.2.   Behavior contract for Jamal. (From Knoster, T. [2014]. *The teacher's pocket guide for effective classroom management* [2nd ed., p. 127]. Baltimore, MD: Paul H. Brookes Publishing Co.; adapted by permission.)

Behavior Contract

Student: <u>Carl O'Malley</u>   Today's date: <u>2/8/16</u>

Student's grade/teacher: <u>7th grade / John Simms</u>

Relevant staff: <u>John Simms, Jane Goode (special educator), Cara Simpson (school</u>

<u>psychologist), Bob Pevey (paraeducator), Isham Tambray (PBIS team leader)</u>

Target behavior (behavioral expectation):

Be respectful: Use appropriate language.

One person speaks at a time.

Listen and follow directions the first time.

Speak only at appropriate times; listen to others when they speak.

Use an indoor voice when speaking.

Data collection procedure:
Use a Good Behavior Chart with + marks for appropriate behavior and – marks for inappropriate behavior. Teachers/staff and Carl independently evaluate his behavior twice per class period (halfway and at end of each class) across five class periods.

Reinforcement procedure (what and how often):
Carl can choose from the Choice Box, which contains items of interest such as a homework pass and a coupon for 10 minutes of extra computer time, at the end of each day when he has earned 7 of 10 + marks.

What must the student do to earn reinforcement?

Be respectful: Use appropriate language.

One person speaks at a time.

Listen and follow directions the first time.

Speak only at appropriate times; listen to others when they are speaking.

Use an indoor voice when speaking.

Criterion: 7 of 10 + marks earned each day.

Consequences for failure to meet behavioral expectations:
Carl will not earn access to the Choice Box. Other relevant consequences may be implemented as deemed appropriate or necessary by Carl's teacher(s).

Bonus for exceptional behavioral performance:
When Carl meets expectations 5 consecutive days in a row, he may make a random choice from the Grand Prize Box, which contains items such as coupons to the local sandwich shop, a free movie pass, and a coupon for one free movie or game rental. When Carl earns two consecutive bonus picks (10 days in a row at 7 of 10 + marks), we will renegotiate the contract.

Signatures of all stakeholders:

_____

_____

_____

_____

Figure 5.3.   Behavior contract for Carl. (From Knoster, T. [2014]. *The teacher's pocket guide for effective classroom management* [2nd ed., p. 127]. Baltimore, MD: Paul H. Brookes Publishing Co.; adapted by permission.)

Good Behavior Chart

Student: <u>Jamal Hall</u>   Staff: <u>Jill Blaine and Corey Smith</u>   Date: <u>2/8/16</u>

Directions: Indicate ☺ for appropriate behavior and ⊗ for inappropriate behavior. Then, tally the morning, afternoon, and daily totals as applicable.

Expectation	Morning		Afternoon	
Be responsible:	☺	☹	☺	☹
• Focus on your work.	☺	☹	☺	☹
• Follow directions the first time.	☺	☹	☺	☹
• Organize and get to work promptly.	☺	☹	☺	☹
• Make a good effort.	☺	☹	☺	☹
Daily total (☺)	_____		_____	/ 10

Figure 5.4. Good Behavior Chart for Jamal. (From Knoster, T. [2014]. *The teacher's pocket guide for effective classroom management* [2nd ed., p. 124]. Baltimore, MD: Paul H. Brookes Publishing Co.; adapted by permission.)

Good Behavior Chart

Student: Carl O'Malley

Date: 2/8/16

Staff: John Simms, Jane Goode, Cara Simpson, Bob Pevey, Isham Tambray

Directions: Indicate + for appropriate behavior and − for inappropriate behavior. Then, tally the period and daily totals as applicable.

Be respectful:	Use appropriate language. One person speaks at a time. Listen and follow directions the first time. Speak only at appropriate times; listen to others when they speak. Use an indoor voice when speaking.					
	First half		Second half		Period total (+)		
Period 1	+	−	+	−	0 1 2
Period 2	+	−	+	−	0 1 2
Period 3	+	−	+	−	0 1 2
Period 4	+	−	+	−	0 1 2
Period 5	+	−	+	−	0 1 2
			Daily total (+)		/10

Figure 5.5. Good Behavior Chart for Carl. (From Knoster, T. [2014]. *The teacher's pocket guide for effective classroom management* [2nd ed., p. 125]. Baltimore, MD: Paul H. Brookes Publishing Co.; adapted by permission.)

he earns an additional bonus reward and you renegotiate the contract (e.g., perhaps shift criterion for performance to nine out of ten per day). All of this is documented in the behavior contract so there is a record of the behavioral intervention. The data are recorded on the behavior chart for easy data collection (see Figures 5.4 and 5.5 for Jamal's and Carl's example charts). There is no set formula to determine exactly when to taper/wean the student from the contract. Rather, this requires professional judgment based on your knowledge of the student and your classroom, coupled with practical realities of time and energy on your part and the student's rate of progress and current levels of performance.

In short, an effective behavior contract has more to do with reinforcement procedures for appropriate behavior than it has to do with negative consequences for inappropriate behavior (given that you select meaningful reinforcement procedures for the student in question). Behavior contracts can be used effectively to teach new skills and reinforce desired behaviors.

CONCLUSION

In summary, teachers in traditional schools have a variety of targeted (Tier 2) supports to consider. We encourage you to consider each of the five options previously described in this chapter when you are choosing targeted supports to put into place for a student. Think especially about feasibility (Can I reasonably put this into place?), consistency (Can I follow through?), and effectiveness (Can I implement this with fidelity over time?). It is important to bear in mind what is already in place that can be built upon and how to continue to create collaborative endeavors with others in your school to support students.

6

How Do You Adjust Targeted Supports Based on Student Progress?

Progress monitoring is a large part of the process for providing effective and efficient targeted supports to improve outcomes for your students. In Chapter 3, we discussed different forms of data that you might collect and use for screening and progress monitoring. In this chapter, we go into more detail about how to use those data to make informed decisions as you taper or change supports, as well as what the process for tapering or changing supports looks like.

THE IMPORTANCE OF VISUAL REPRESENTATIONS OF DATA

One of the first considerations in putting your data to use is to express it in a format that is quickly understandable. This will help you to recognize patterns to inform your teaching, as well as give you a user-friendly manner to share your interpretation of the information you have collected with parents and colleagues. This should prove helpful both in delivering the targeted supports as well as adjusting supports over time.

We illustrate this using what has become an all-too-familiar experience. In a meeting regarding behavioral concerns, Shawn's teacher took out the original data sheet that she recorded on in class that day. She shared this snapshot with Shawn's mother to show what a typical day looked like for Shawn. The problem was the data sheet was just that: a data sheet with a list of codes and numbers. The data sheet appeared to Shawn's mother as if it was written in a foreign language. Shawn's mother just sat back in her seat and sighed.

Representing data graphically (visually) helps everyone to make meaning of the information. Graphic displays help you and others to see patterns, such as when behavior occurs (e.g., time, date), how often it occurs (e.g., frequency, percentage, rate), the type of behavior (e.g., prosocial behavior, problem behavior), the trend in the behavior (e.g., increasing, decreasing, no change), and the level of behavior (e.g., the degree of change in the form of how much the behavior increased or decreased). Analyzing these types of patterns through visual displays can help you and others make instructional decisions.

> Data are usually most understandable and useful when expressed visually.

Analyzing Data in a PBIS Context

Schools implementing PBIS will likely already have procedures to gather useful data at the school level, which will take some of the burden off you as the teacher. Relevant data will be collected and typically analyzed at the school and classroom level by your school's universal and advanced tier teams. For example, as described in prior chapters, student attendance and ODRs are typically monitored in a PBIS school. You are encouraged to graphically display this readily available information.

To illustrate, let's say that Shawn has been increasingly coming late to class. This has occurred on more than a couple of occasions during the last few weeks. Tardiness data are tracked by the office, and the data are aggregated on a scheduled basis (typically monthly or quarterly) for review by the universal prevention team. As a teacher in this school, you have access to a printout of how many tardies each student in your class has had per week within each reporting period. In turn, you can graphically display the average tardies in a week for Shawn as compared to the other students in your class, as depicted in Figure 6.1. By looking at this graph, it is easy to see that Shawn's tardies are occurring at a rate significantly higher than the class average. Comparing charts like this before, during, and after implementing targeted supports addressing his tardiness can be a quick indicator of whether the supports are effective.

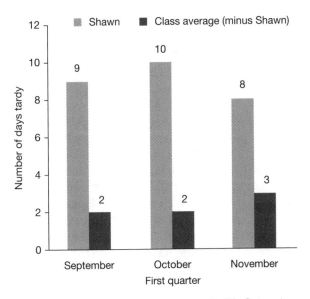

Figure 6.1. Shawn's number of tardies per month of the first quarter.

Visual displays of data that are relevant to targeted supports may already be available to you, depending on the software program used in your PBIS School (e.g., SWIS). Based on your needs, you may also create additional visual displays of data to facilitate decision making associated with targeted support.

Analyzing Data in a Classroom in a Traditional School

In schools not implementing PBIS, data collection and analysis are likely still routine aspects of school operations. However, with regard to student behavior concerns, the processes may occur more on a case-by-case basis. For example, in one school, the second and third graders share the playground at recess; here, a few students have been identified as needing targeted support in social skills based on the fact that the recess assistant has repeatedly directed them to sit on the side of the playground due to problem behavior. The guidance counselor has started targeted social skills training sessions for this small group of students and has continued to collect data on these students' behavior via the recess assistant. The data were reviewed by the second- and third-grade teams.

The graph in Figure 6.2 shows the data in a 2-week period displayed by each day. The teachers can easily see how many students sat on the side of the playground for each recess period by viewing the graph. Furthermore, visual inspection of these data help to clarify that problems are equally common for students in both grades and that the trend in the data indicates a decrease. Fewer students are required to sit on the side of the playground from Monday to Friday; on the last 2 days of each week, there were no students sitting out. This graph is helpful to the teachers to see a clear decreasing pattern to the point that no students were being asked to sit out due to inappropriate play behaviors by the end of each week.

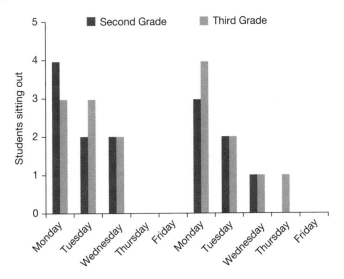

Figure 6.2. Students sitting on the side of the playground at recess across a 2-week period.

IDENTIFYING AND HIGHLIGHTING THE MOST RELEVANT DATA

How do you decide what information is important to graphically display? We address this question based on the presumption that you have put into practice the data gathering procedures we previously described in Chapter 3. There are two pieces of critical information to consider at this point. Refer back to your goal for the student(s) and how you decided to collect data on the effect of the selected targeted supports. Remember, you identified the data you would collect when you decided how to assess your targeted supports on your resource map.

Let's go back to Tyler's example and his goal of participation in PE to illustrate. Tyler was acting out because he was having squabbles with other students during games. As we described previously, the teacher decided to record data concerning Tyler's participation for the entire period. In graphing this information (Figure 6.3), each column represented a week; over the course of 6 weeks, the graph depicts for each week the percentage of days out of 5 that Tyler participated for the entire class period. Therefore, as Tyler's behavior improves in response to targeted supports, there will be an increasing trend and increasing level (e.g., successful participation moving up from 2 days to 4 days, as depicted in Figure 6.3). You could represent the data weekly as explained or monthly.

The primary condition that makes data meaningful (or functional) is its use. Targeted support data should be reviewed on an ongoing basis to see a larger picture that reflects student progress. One helpful strategy that we encourage you to employ with your visually displayed data is to place an aim line on the graph. An aim line is created by drawing a line from the baseline data point (or beginning point of intervention) to the goal point. For example, perhaps the goal for Rob, who is receiving peer mediation in tandem with a self-monitoring checklist, is to increase his engagement in working during class from 5 minutes up to 20 minutes out of a 30-minute class period each day within the next 2 weeks. Both the teacher and Rob monitor his engagement during this time. Each day, the teacher's data are graphed and tracked in relationship to the aim line (Figure 6.4).

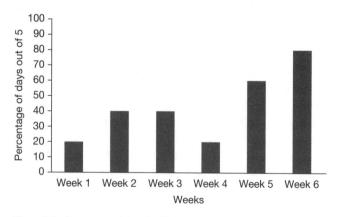

Figure 6.3. Percentage of time that Tyler participated in gym class each week.

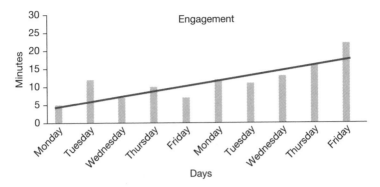

Figure 6.4. Setting an aim line to compare Rob's progress compared with goal for increased classroom engagement over a 2-week period.

There are three considerations to make when interpreting these data about Rob. First, to determine his responsiveness to the targeted support, view Rob's data in relation to the goal of 20 minutes of engagement. You can determine if Rob is getting closer to the goal based on the trend of the graph line (the line going up or down). Second, looking at the amount of the change (level) can help to determine to what degree Rob's engagement is improving over time. Third, the data can be judged for consistency to determine if Rob's behavior is becoming more or less predictable. Given these three considerations, you are now ready to use the information gleaned to inform your practice.

The key question becomes whether Rob is sufficiently responding to the targeted supports. If the answer is yes, then a logical decision would be that the Tier 2 intervention continues, unless you are at the point in time to consider fading the targeted support. However, if the answer is no, then you are encouraged to look at the data and goal again to determine what changes need to be made. As can be seen in Rob's case, sufficient progress is being realized.

> Use your data to determine whether a student is sufficiently responding to targeted supports.

WHAT MIGHT THE DATA LOOK LIKE, AND HOW DO WE MOVE FORWARD?

When progress is being realized (e.g., as with Rob), the student is making consistent progress or has reached the goal. In this situation, the decision becomes whether to continue with the intervention as currently being implemented or whether sufficient progress has been realized to fade the intervention. The decision in Rob's case might be to continue the intervention in its current form or to change the intervention in some way. This change may be part of a fading process or may become a form of sustained support for the student. Fading the intensity of the intervention in a systematic way can help to ease the student into a more independent phase of performance. The fading of targeted supports should be intentional, gradual, and guided by your data. For example, in reviewing Rob's data on engagement, he appears to have been very responsive to a combination of peer mediation and use of a self-monitoring checklist. In light of his progress, you might decide to fade the peer intervention and continue with the self-monitoring checklist for another 2 weeks.

What Does It Look Like When a Student Appears Unresponsive, and What Should You Do?

The data may appear to trend opposite of the desired direction, show little or no growth in level, or may reflect a great degree of inconsistency when students appear unresponsive to targeted support. For example, the student's time on task (shown in Figure 6.5) is inconsistent and features no growth across 2 weeks of a targeted support being implemented. This may be an indicator that changes are needed to the targeted support. As a first step, when the data reflect inconsistent or incomplete patterns, we encourage you to explore other data sources, such as teacher or administrator report, behavioral screeners, and progress monitoring tools that may help tell a more complete story.

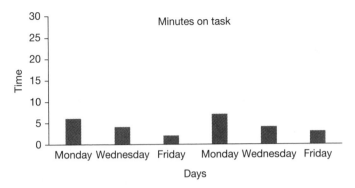

Figure 6.5. Duration of time on task.

Determining what exactly is going on when a student appears unresponsive to a targeted support is key to determining what actions to take. Was the support being implemented as intended? Are there other factors (e.g., health, family issues) that may have contributed to the student's apparent lack of progress? In other words, investigate what is occurring in order to determine whether you need to and how you can vary the type or intensity of the targeted support. You may decide to change the intervention in some way, such as the degree of intensity through time/amount (longer or shorter sessions), frequency (more or less opportunities), content delivery (more explicit instructions), and/or content application (different skills for better alignment to your student's needs). In addition, consider if there are different support options or additional tools that may help the student make reasonable progress. A short or abbreviated version of a functional behavior assessment, such as the Functional Assessment Checklist for Teachers and Staff (FACTS; McIntosh et al., 2008), may also be worth consideration at this point in time. If there continues to be a lack of sufficient response to targeted supports, you may need to consider individualized intensive (Tier 3) supports, which are discussed in a bit more detail in Chapter 7.

For an example of how a student's supports can be adjusted as time goes by, let's take another look at Samuel, the third grader who was introduced in Chapter 1 and highlighted in Chapter 4. He increasingly needed redirection from the teacher regarding the expectations on the playground, and his problem behavior had increased to include physically pushing others and throwing tantrums. However, it was also found that he helped other students to work together as long as conflict did not involve him directly. Samuel's reading skills fell in the low range for third grade. The Tier 2 team created a plan to meet Samuel's needs. First, the guidance counselor included Samuel in a problem-based learning group, where students took turns in a leadership role and worked through team-based problems. Samuel learned skills that would help him to work with others in a variety of situations. In addition, Samuel met biweekly with a third-grade peer mentor to help with reading and work on accountability with meeting school expectations.

The Tier 2 team viewed the data collected for Samuel, including frequency of redirection provided by the teacher, ODRs during recess, and duration of time on task during group activities. The results indicated that ODRs decreased and time on task increased during group work, but the frequency of redirection remained high at other times. As the team looked more closely at the data, it seemed that redirection occurred after longer periods of time listening or engaging in one activity. The team decided to add a component to teach Samuel to ask for a break after a certain amount of work was completed. Assignments were subsequently chunked. When Samuel met the expectation of completing the chunk, he then could ask for a short break prior to returning to his work task.

USING A TEAM TO DEVELOP AND SUSTAIN TARGETED SUPPORTS

A team approach is ideal when providing targeted supports to students. It is efficient for schools to bring together a common team that has expertise in the resources available in the school and community to meet students' diverse needs.

Students who are in need of targeted (Tier 2) support often have a history of problem behavior that can be somewhat ingrained, and a collaborative approach can bring the creativity and innovation necessary to create change. In PBIS schools, various teams are established to support students by viewing goals, analyzing data, and making data-informed decisions concerning prevention and intervention. In more traditional schools, teachers can move to create teams or enhance existing teams to help students in need of targeted supports. Many traditional schools have individualized support teams or student support teams in place that pull together teachers, counselors, interventionists, administrators, and families to plan for students who may require more specialized supports. Such a team may be able to expand its focus to include targeted supports.

> Just as a team (ideally) is involved in identifying and developing targeted supports, a team should be involved in progress monitoring and deciding what comes next.

Targeted support (Tier 2) teams should be involved in an ongoing process of assessment and review of student progress. The team should consider whether students are sufficiently responding to targeted support. Whether you work within a PBIS school (with your Tier 2 team) or in a traditional school (within another form of a school-based team), you are encouraged to evaluate if progress is made and when tapering can occur, if progress is being made but the targeted support should remain in its current form, or if more intensive support is needed. These adjustments can be made at the targeted support (Tier 2) level, although you may need to consider additional supports as needed based on student response.

CONCLUSION

By nature, targeted supports involve an end date—a time by which it is hoped the support will no longer be needed. When monitoring progress to determine how well a support is work-ing, keep in mind that if it has been successful, eventually the support should be tapered; if it is not, successful changes can and should be made.

In some cases, by watching how a student responds (or does not respond) to a targeted support, you and your team may determine the student is a candidate for individualized intensive supports. These Tier 3 supports should only be nec-essary for a very few students with particularly challenging behavior. Although developing such supports requires further expertise, greater collaboration, and many considerations beyond the scope of this book, we believe you should have a sense of what this level looks like. Therefore, Chapter 7 covers the basics of individualized intensive supports.

7

How Do Targeted Supports Relate to Individualized Intensive Supports?

There will likely be a small portion of students in any given school who may not sufficiently respond to targeted supports—even really well-designed and well-implemented targeted supports. Given this reality, we would be remiss if we failed to provide some reasonable degree of guidance concerning individualized intensive (Tier 3) supports. Before we get into the details of such supports, we start by emphasizing what we believe to be the single most important thing for you as a teacher to keep in clear view when it comes to this next level of support: Designing and implementing effective individualized intensive supports that not only address needs and concerns in the short term but also lead to meaningful outcomes that are sustainable over time requires a collaborative team approach. Regardless of how great a teacher you may be, this is the honest, blunt truth. No teacher will have enough wherewithal or resiliency to be able to provide all of the supports needed without the help of others. Therefore, you need to work within available teaming structures at your school (e.g., advanced tier teams if you happen to teach within a PBIS school). If such teaming structures are not readily available in your school, you are encouraged to start by recruiting others into a team process in as time efficient a manner as possible. Logically, if the student of concern receives special education, the IEP team should serve as the student-centered team, as was also noted in Chapter 4 concerning targeted supports. However, not all students requiring individualized intensive supports will have identified disabilities. In the event that no teaming structure is currently available, you may need to establish a team through your own efforts by talking with your building administrator.

Beyond the importance of teaming, we would also be remiss if we did not provide guidance to you as to how to interpret the following material in this chapter. The term *individualized intensive* is a pretty fair description of the nature of this level of support. It requires individualizing supports to a given student's needs and situation (see Table 7.1 for examples of such student characteristics and scenarios), and it is more intensive than the targeted supports described in this book. This chapter provides a conceptual overview of what is typically required when providing this level of support. However, if you may be providing individualized intensive supports to a student, you will need much more knowledge about the foundations, processes, and range of practices than what we present here. You are highly encouraged to explore additional resources, such as those we have listed in the Resources.

PLANNING AND IMPLEMENTING INDIVIDUALIZED INTENSIVE SUPPORT

Providing individualized intensive supports can feel like a complex process, which is part of why it is so critical to address it as a team. Although not required, having a structure in place or a specific model to follow can also be helpful to guide the team's work and ensure that they provide support in a manner

Table 7.1. Considerations for determining when individualized intensive support is warranted

Characteristics and context	How this might play out in the classroom
The student's problem behavior persists despite consistently implemented classroom-based supports.	Despite the student having been exposed to well-designed and implemented universal prevention within the classroom management structure, in tandem with the layering on of targeted supports within the school, he or she is still engaging in problem behavior.
The student's problem behavior places the student or others at risk of harm, exclusion, or devaluation by others.	The student is engaging in behavior that has a high probability of resulting in physical or emotional injury. This injury or harm could be to the student engaging in the behavior of concern or others in the immediate environment (e.g., other students, staff, volunteers). Furthermore, the behavior of concern may be resulting in the student being removed from the typical classroom setting or classmates not being present in the classroom. Additionally, the student engaging in the problem behavior may be perceived by others (e.g., classmates, staff, volunteers) as undesirable to be around or someone to be avoided.
Personnel are considering more intrusive or invasive procedures and/or a more restrictive educational placement.	School and/or other agency staff involved with the student or caregivers are increasingly frustrated or fearful and may be considering (or perhaps already using) increasingly punitive approaches that may include even physical restraint. Additionally, school staff are considering more restrictive educational placement options as a direct result of concerns about the student's problem behavior.

From Bambara, L.M., & Knoster, T. (2009). *Designing positive behavior support plans.* Washington, DC: American Association on Intellectual and Developmental Disabilities; reprinted by permission.

that is grounded in scientific evidence. One promising school-based model of individualized behavior support for students in kindergarten through eighth grade is known as Prevent-Teach-Reinforce (PTR; Dunlap et al., 2010). The model has proven to be user friendly and involves five steps: teaming, goal setting, assessment, intervention, and evaluation. There are various resource materials available that detail each step

> Individualized intensive support requires a person-centered team's involvement and entails a more systematic approach than targeted or universal supports.

of PTR, as well as other organizational frameworks to support you in providing individualized intensive supports, such as FACTS (as mentioned in Chapter 6) and the Functional Assessment Interview (FAI; O'Neill et al., 2014). A number of these resources are noted in the Resources section of this book for your convenience. Regardless of whether you employ PTR or some other compatible approach, this chapter should provide you with a sufficient understanding of the seminal components of providing individualized intensive support.

Key Principles of Individualized Intensive Support

There are four guiding principles that should govern the design and delivery of individualized intensive support. First, it is important to understand that problem behavior of any student is context related. Second, keep in mind that the student's behavior—regardless of how odd or concerning it may appear—serves a function for the student. Third, never lose sight of the fact that effective individualized intensive supports are based on a thorough understanding of the student, his or her social contexts, and the function of the problem behavior. Last, but by no means least important, you are encouraged to remember that individualized intensive support should be grounded in person-centered values that respect the dignity, preferences, and aspirations of the student.

Keeping these four guiding principles in mind, let's turn our attention to the three major stages of providing individualized intensive supports. Table 7.2 depicts these three interrelated stages in the team process of providing this level of support.

Table 7.2. Three interrelated stages of individualized intensive support

Stage	Highlights
Functional behavioral assessment (FBA)	The team identifies what problem behavior is of greatest concern and, in turn, operationally defines the behavior in terms of what it looks and/or sounds like. The team next determines how best to go about gathering broad and specific information about the student, his or her problem behavior, and various social contexts in the student's typical daily routine. Additionally, the team should consider the relevance of concurrently engaging in some form of person-centered planning to address broader life circumstances of the student (e.g., employing what is often described as a wraparound approach). The team analyzes the information that it has gathered and formulates a specific and global hypothesis statement concerning the student and his or her problem behavior. The team uses these hypotheses to develop the multicomponent behavior support plan.
Design and implementation of multicomponent behavior support plan	The team will collaboratively brainstorm and select strategies to a) prevent problem behavior in the short term, b) teach alternative skills to the student, c) reinforce acquisition and use of the alternative skills (as well as design ways to respond to problem behavior so as to not inadvertently reinforce the occurrence of the problem behavior), and d) prevent problem behavior over the longer term. The selection of the strategies to be employed across these four component parts of the behavior support plan should align with the hypotheses developed through the FBA as well as be acceptable to those who will be required to implement the behavior support plan. The collection of data for the purposes of progress monitoring should also be built into the behavior support plan. The team should, at least periodically, discuss issues impacting implementation of the behavior support plan with fidelity.
Evaluation via progress monitoring of effectiveness of the behavior support plan	Data are gathered throughout implementation of the behavior support plan. Emphasis is placed on tracking the impact of the behavior support plan on a) reductions in problem behavior, b) increases in use of alternative skills, and c) impact on quality of life for the student, family, and other relevant parties, including the staff. These data are used within the context of periodic team meetings to inform decision making about adjusting component parts of the behavior support plan over time.

From Bambara, L.M., & Knoster, T. (2009). *Designing positive behavior support plans*. Washington, DC: American Association on Intellectual and Developmental Disabilities; reprinted by permission.

Functional Behavioral Assessment

Conducting a functional behavioral assessment (FBA) involves prioritizing and operationally defining the problem behavior of concern. When operationally defining the problem behavior, ask the question: "What does the student look like or sound like when engaging in the behavior of concern?" Asking this question will help you to define the problem behavior using verbs that will assist in gathering and analyzing two types of information: broad and specific. Broad information reflects important contextual information about the student, including strengths and interests, general history, skill deficits, and the goals for the student in tandem with perspective from the student and his or her family concerning quality of life (e.g., relationships, basic needs, age-appropriate opportunities to make choices). Specific information reflects precise and detailed information about what triggers the student to engage in problem behavior (antecedents), what the actual problem looks/sounds like (behavior), and what the student gets or avoids as a result of the problem behavior (consequences, or function). Your team will need to determine the most time-efficient methods for gathering both types of information.

> The results of the functional behavioral assessment (FBA) should lead your team to hypotheses about why the student engages in the problem behavior(s), which in turn will guide your plan for individualized behavior support.

Once both types of information have been gathered and analyzed, your team should summarize the results of the FBA into global and specific hypothesis statements. These hypotheses, regardless of the degree of broad and specific information gathered throughout the FBA, are simply informed conjecture as to why the student engages in the problem behavior(s). These hypothesis statements serve as a navigational device for your team to design the multicomponent behavior support plan. Table 7.3 provides some example hypothesis statements.

Table 7.3. Specific and global hypothesis statements for Michael

Specific hypothesis	Global hypothesis
When Michael is presented with academic tasks that require extensive writing, independent academic assignments that appear complex to the degree that Michael feels overwhelmed, or individual academic work that requires more than 15 minutes to complete, Michael will get out of his assigned seat, use profanity with the teacher as well as other students, and tear up his material to avoid completing the assigned task.	Michael is a 13-year-old eighth-grade student who appears interested in what most other boys his age in the community find of interest. He particularly likes auto racing and goes to watch his uncle race on the dirt track in his hometown every weekend. Michael really enjoys working on engines of any type and has excellent hand–eye coordination as well as manual dexterity. He lives with his mother and father and has an older brother, who is also into dirt track racing, attends the local technical school, and is studying automotive repair. Michael is identified as having emotional disturbance and a learning disability in reading (his reading is around the fifth-grade level based on curriculum-based measures). He receives most of his academic instruction in the general education classroom with the exception of receiving pull-out special education supports for English. Michael is interested in attending the local technical school; however, he expresses both concern and frustration about his chances of being admitted to the technical school given his academic difficulties and growing disciplinary record at school. Michael has been sent to the office as a result of his increasing degree of problem behavior during this marking period (i.e., six office discipline referrals this period alone). He also gets upset when he perceives other students' actions as indicating that they think he is "stupid" (to quote Michael). At this stage, Michael thinks it is better to be viewed by his classmates and teachers as "bad" as opposed to not being capable of successfully completing assignments.

Multicomponent Behavior Support Plan

A behavior support plan for a student in need of individualized intensive supports should be comprised of numerous intervention and support strategies. Typically, no one strategy or support in isolation will result in meaningful and sustainable results. Furthermore, to be efficient and effective, the behavior support plan must also fit the student's environmental and social contexts. Your team should use the specific and global hypothesis statements to guide the selection and implementation of the behavior support plan. The individual intervention and support strategies included in the plan can be considered to fall into categories of short-term prevention of problem behavior, teaching alternative skills, reinforcing acquisition and use of the alternative skills, and long-term prevention of problem behavior.

Short-Term Prevention of Problem Behavior   Short-term prevention strategies (sometimes referred to as *antecedent strategies* or *setting event strategies*) reflect ways in which the staff will rearrange environmental conditions at school to address the fast triggers noted in the specific hypothesis. There are a variety of ways in which staff can address fast triggers at school. These include removing triggering events, modifying triggering events, blocking/neutralizing triggering events, interspersing desired or easier tasks with less desired or instructional level tasks, and adding access to preferred things (stimuli) to enhance student engagement in tasks. A behavior support plan should reflect some combination of these five types of short-term prevention strategies. Use of these types of strategies should have a fast, positive impact on reducing the frequency of problem behavior. However, in isolation, short-term prevention will prove insufficient for two reasons. First, the student of concern is not being taught any new, alternative skills. Second, even if you wanted to, it is impossible to control exposure to triggers all of the time.

Teaching Alternative Skills   Teaching alternative skills requires your team to identify and teach to mastery of three skills in different yet related areas. These include a replacement behavior to serve the same function as the problem behavior as noted in the specific hypothesis, multiple general skills that address the skill deficits reflected in the global hypothesis, and coping/self-calming skills that will enable the student to be able to work through reasonably stressful situations without reverting to problem behavior. It is important that your team target and teach to mastery skills across each of these three domains to best ensure short-term and long-term positive results. Teaching a replacement behavior requires targeting a socially acceptable way in which the student of concern can gain access to the same function of the problem behavior (e.g., replacing swearing and tearing up materials to escape the difficult task with raising one's hand and saying, "I need help or a break"). General skills are simply a broad set of skills that alter problem situations and prevent the need for problem behavior (e.g., teaching a student organizational skills for breaking down what appear to be complex directions into smaller, more digestible steps). Coping skills require direct instruction in ways in which the student of concern can calm down when feeling frustrated or upset (e.g., closing one's eyes and taking three deep breaths). When identifying skills to instruct, priority should be placed on skills that most easily generalize, or transfer, across multiple settings (e.g., in various classrooms, at home, in the community).

Reinforcement and Consequences   Your team will also need to plan strategies regarding how staff members respond to behavior, both in terms of reinforcement when the student acquires and uses the alternative skill and in terms of consequences if undesired behavior arises again in the future. When designing reinforcement procedures associated with alternative skills, it is important to think in the short term (initial skill acquisition) and long term (maintenance over time in the use of the alternative skill once it is initially acquired). Reinforcement during the acquisition stage should be delivered immediately or as close to the occurrence of the targeted behavior as possible and should be consistently delivered as the student demonstrates the desired behavior. Once the student has acquired the alternative skill(s), which requires a judgment call on the part of you as the teacher, you may then begin to shift the schedule of reinforcement to a more intermittent and/or delayed schedule (e.g., delaying how fast you respond to the student's hand raising in the classroom once hand raising is acquired).

Responding to inappropriate behavior also requires decision making by the team in the design process of the behavior support plan. Nuisance-level behavior should generally be systematically ignored unless it persists for too long (e.g., simple off-task behavior for 15 seconds as compared with off-task behavior bordering closer to 45 seconds). Ideally, while ignoring the nuisance behavior, you should provide reinforcement to another student who is engaging in appropriate behavior in close proximity to the student engaged in the nuisance behavior, as done with universal-level classroom management.

For problem behavior, which should not be ignored, you will want to design into the behavior support plan the use of stop-redirect procedures that are also compatible with direct intervention procedures associated with universal-level classroom management. The primary focus with redirection procedures is to not inadvertently reinforce occurrence of the problem behavior (e.g., using a time-out procedure for a student engaged in escape motivated behavior) as well as to redirect the student to engage in appropriate behavior in the most time-efficient manner possible. Furthermore, a crisis management plan should be built in to the student's behavior support plan when warranted.

Long-Term Prevention of Problem Behavior   Long-term prevention is the fourth major component of an individualized behavior support plan. Long-term prevention is comprised of strategies to support maintenance and generalization of the targeted alternative skills, increasing opportunities for choice and decision making, supportive approaches that may be required to address any health related concerns, and strategies to facilitate relationship building based on interests of the student. Collectively, these strategies and supports contribute to the long-term prevention of problem behavior through the general improvement in the student's quality of life. Meaningful participation and inclusion at school and in the community can be achieved through long-term prevention. Outcomes associated with long-term prevention tend to also be the types of outcomes that resonate the most with the student of concern and his or her family (e.g., increased friendships with classmates, the family's ability to successfully attend community-based activities). Building on Table 7.3, Table 7.4 provides examples of strategies and supports for Michael in terms of short-term prevention, alternative skills, consequence strategies, and long-term prevention.

Table 7.4. Strategies and supports for Michael

Short-term prevention	Give Michael alternatives to writing to complete tasks (e.g., providing verbal or typed responses).
	Break tasks into smaller units to keep independent tasks to no longer than 10 minutes.
	When Michael is required to complete multistep tasks, break directions into smaller, bite-size chunks and incorporate auto racing themes.
	When independent tasks are required of Michael, provide encouragement by increasing the frequency of staff reinforcement for effort.
	Intersperse (alternate) easy tasks with more difficult tasks at Michael's instructional level across subject areas whenever feasible.
Alternative skills	Replacement behavior • Teach Michael to raise his hand to request a short break (e.g., to get a drink of water) when he feels overwhelmed or frustrated.
	General skills • Increase Michael's reading skills over time. • Improve Michael's writing skills over time. • Teach Michael social problem-solving skills to use when confronted with situations that create stress for him in the presence of other classmates (e.g., stop-think-act strategies).
	Coping skills • Teach Michael to take three deep breaths before responding to a peer's statement or body language/eye contact that Michael believes is not positive.

(continued)

Table 7.4. (*continued*)

Consequence strategies	Reinforcing alternative skills • During the acquisition of alternative skills, provide behavior-specific praise for Michael's use of the alternative skills and allow a break for his use of the replacement behavior of raising his hand to request a break. • Once Michael has mastered the alternative skills, his continued successful use of them will result in increased achievement and positive outcomes, accompanied by a greater sense of power and self-control on Michael's part. Responding to inappropriate behavior • Use planned ignoring for low-level nuisance behavior. • Use stop-redirect-reinforce procedures for problem behavior, redirecting Michael to use his replacement and/or coping skills.
Long-term prevention	Maintenance and generalization of alternative skills • Once alternative skills are mastered, foster skill maintenance by shifting the schedule of reinforcement to an intermittent schedule. • Foster generalization by providing behavior-specific praise for use of the alternative skills across settings. Choice opportunities • Increasingly incorporate choices into tasks to be completed as feasible (e.g., provide a choice in the task completion sequence when multiple assignments are required). Relationships and community • Work with Michael to explore involvement in student activities and community-based experiences based on his interests (e.g., the local racetrack). • Explore with Michael involvement in community-based volunteer activities related to his interests (e.g., working with the local repair garage to provide repairs to neighbors with limited financial means).

PROGRESS MONITORING AND EVALUATION OF IMPACT

There are three important outcomes for which data should be gathered and used to monitor progress when delivering individualized intensive support: 1) reductions in problem behavior, 2) acquisition and use of socially acceptable alternative

Table 7.5. Questions for the team to ask if there is insufficient progress being realized with the student, and corresponding actions to take.

Question	Likely team actions
Has sufficient time been provided for the support plan to have the desired effect?	Review timelines and adjust as needed.
Are the strategies and supports explicitly linked to the hypothesis statements that summarized the results of the FBA?	Review all strategies and supports to assure they are addressing triggers, skill development and the function of the student's problem behavior, and adjust as needed.
Is the behavior support plan, in its entirety, being implemented with fidelity?	Discuss among team members implementation of the behavior support plan and conduct observations for purposes of fidelity checks across settings if warranted. Also, re-visit discussion among team members of contextual fit and identify and provide supports to team members as needed.
Has something changed in the student's life circumstances that have made the hypothesis statements you previously developed no longer accurate?	Review among team members the hypothesis statements your team formed to make sure that they accurately summarize the FBA data. Also consider if any new important developments have recently occurred for the student. Gather additional information and re-develop hypothesis statements as needed.
Are the strategies and supports sufficiently effective?	Review among team members the student progress data to determine if the prevention strategies are having the desired effect, along with considering if the alternative skills are proving effective and efficient for the student (especially focus on the impact of both type and frequency of reinforcement associated with the alternative skills), and revise the plan as needed.
Are student and family interests and preferences reflected in the behavior support plan, especially in terms of long-term prevention and socially valid targeted outcomes?	Discuss among team members the degree of student and parent satisfaction with the process of delivery and resultant outcomes of the behavior support plan, and revise the plan as needed.

From Bambara, L.M., & Knoster, T. (2009). *Designing positive behavior support plans*. Washington, DC: American Association on Intellectual and Developmental Disabilities; reprinted by permission.

Key: FBA, functional behavioral assessment.

skills, and 3) enhancements to quality of life. Data collection procedures similar to those used throughout the FBA may also be used in gathering data for the purposes of monitoring progress. In a parallel fashion to targeted support, these data should be used by the student-centered team in making decisions about changes in the behavior support plan based on student progress over time. Reaching a consensus with the student and his or her family on establishing meaningful outcomes is an important aspect of providing individualized intensive supports. As was the case with certain targeted supports, this may also require collaboration with members of the extended team to reflect staff from other child-serving systems who also are working with the student and his or her family. Clarifying commonly shared goals and targeted outcomes can greatly facilitate the process of providing this level of tiered supports.

It is possible that data may show insufficient progress in any or all of the outcomes noted previously. In the event sufficient progress is not being realized while implementing a behavior support plan, Table 7.5 offers a series of questions that a student-centered team may find helpful for interpreting such findings and planning what to try next.

CONCLUSION

This final chapter presented a quick overview of what is required to provide individualized intensive supports for a student who does not sufficiently respond to universal and targeted supports. This quick overview is just that—a quick overview. We have not delved into extensive depth on FBA or multicomponent support plans, nor have we provided guidance on incorporating the practices described in concert with broader person-centered planning (e.g., wraparound approaches). We highly encourage exploring additional resources and guidance in the event that you need to initiate the design and delivery of these supports. In the Individualized Intensive (Tier 3) Supports section of the Resources, we provide user-friendly resources on conducting an FBA and, in turn, on designing a behavior support plan for a particular student.

References

Anderson, C.M., & Borgmeier, C. (2010). Tier II interventions within the framework of school-wide positive behavior support: Essential features for design, implementation and maintenance. *Behavioral Analysis in Practice, 3*(1), 33–45.

Bambara, L.M., & Knoster, T. (2009). *Designing positive behavior support plans.* Washington, DC: American Association on Intellectual and Developmental Disabilities.

Brown, F., Anderson, J.L., & DePry, R.L. (2015). *Individual positive behavior supports: A standards-based guide to practices in school and community settings.* Baltimore, MD: Paul H. Brookes Publishing Co.

Campbell, A., & Anderson, C.M. (2008). Enhancing effects of Check-In/Check-Out with function-based support. *Behavioral Disorders, 33*(4), 233–245.

Chafouleas, S.M., Riley-Tillman, T.C., & Christ, T.J. (2009). Direct Behavior Rating (DBR): An emerging method for assessing social behavior within a tiered intervention system. *Assessment for Effective Intervention, 34,* 195–200. doi: 10.1177//1534508409340391

Cheney, D., Lynass, L., Flower, A., Waugh, M., Iwaszuk, W., Mielenz, C., & Hawken, L. (2010). The Check, Connect, and Expect Program: A targeted, Tier 2 intervention in the schoolwide positive behavior support model. *Preventing School Failure, 53*(3), 152–158. doi: 10.1080/10459880903492742

Craig, S. (2008). *Reaching and teaching children who hurt: Strategies for your classroom.* Baltimore, MD: Paul H. Brookes Publishing Co.

Crone, D.A., Horner, R.H., & Hawken, L.S. (2004). *Responding to problem behavior in schools: The Behavior Education Program.* New York, NY: Guilford Press.

Danielson, L., & Rosenquist, C. (2014). Introduction to the TEC special issue on data-based individualization. *Council for Exceptional Children, 46*(4), 6–12. doi: 10.1177/004005991452965

Dowd, T., & Tierney, J. (1995). *Boys Town: Teaching social skills to youth.* Boys Town, NE: Boys Town Press.

Drummond, T. (1994). *The Student Risk Screening Scale (SRSS).* Grants Pass, OR: Josephine County Mental Health Program.

Dunlap, G., Iovannone, R., Kincaid, D., Wilson, K., Christiansen, K., Strain, P., & English, C. (2010). *Prevent-Teach-Reinforce: The school-based model of individualized positive behavior support.* Baltimore, MD: Paul H. Brookes Publishing Co.

Dunlap, G., Sailor, W., Horner, R. H., & Sugai, G. (2009). Overview and history of positive behavior support. In W. Sailor, G. Dunlap,

G. Sugai, & R. Horner (Eds.), *Handbook of positive behavior support* (pp. 3–16). New York, NY: Springer.

Elliott, S.N., & Gresham, F.M. (1991) *Social Skills Intervention Guide: Practical Strategies for Social Skills Training.* Circle Pines, MN: American Guidance Service.

Epstein, M. (2004). *Behavioral and Emotional Rating Scale, Second Edition (BERS-2).* Austin, TX: PRO-ED.

Frey, K.S., Nolen, S.B., Edstrom, L.V., & Hirschstein, M.K. (2005). Effects of a school-based social-emotional competence program: Linking children's goals, attributions, and behavior. *Journal of Applied Developmental Psychology, 26,* 171–200.

Goodman, R. (1997). The Strengths and Difficulties Questionnaire: A research note. *Journal of Child Psychology and Psychiatry, 38,* 581–586.

Gresham, F.M., & Elliott, S.N. (2008). *Social Skills Improvement System (SSIS). Rating Scale.* San Antonio, TX: Pearson.

Grossman, D.C., Neckerman, H.J., Koepsell, T.D., Asher, K., Liu, P.Y., Beland, K.N.,...& Rivara, F.P. (1997). A randomized controlled trial of a violence prevention curriculum among elementary school children. *Journal of the American Medical Association, 277,* 1605–1611.

Hawken, L.S., Adolphson, S.L., MacKleod, K.S., & Shumann, J. (2009). Secondary-tier interventions and supports. In W. Sailor, G. Dunlap, G. Suigai, & R. Horner (Eds.), *Handbook of positive behavior support* (pp. 395–420). New York, NY: Springer.

Hawken, L.S., Pettersson, H., Mootz, J., & Anderson, C. (2005). *The Behavior Education Program: A check-in, check-out intervention for students at risk.* New York, NY: Guilford Press.

Horner, R.H., Chard, D.J., Boland, J.B., & Good III, R.H. (2006). The use of reading and behavior screening measures to predict nonresponse to school-wide positive behavior support: A longitudinal analysis. *School Psychology Review, 35*(2), 275–291.

Horner, R.H., Sugai, G., & Anderson, C.M. (2010). Examining the evidence base for school-wide positive behavior support. *Focus on Exceptional Children, 42,* 2–14.

Individuals with Disabilities Education Improvement Act (IDEA) of 2004, PL 108-446, 20 U.S.C. §§ 1400 *et seq.*

Kaminski, R.A., & Good III, R.H. (1998). Assessing early literacy skills in a problem-solving model: Dynamic indicators of basic early literacy skills. In M.R. Shinn (Ed.), *Advanced applications of curriculum-based measurement* (pp. 113–142). New York, NY: Guilford Press.

Kamphaus, R.W., & Reynolds, C.R. (2007). *Behavior Assessment System for Children—Second Edition (BASC-2): Behavioral and Emotional Screening System (BESS).* Bloomington, MN: Pearson.

Kamphaus, R.W., & Reynolds, C.R. (2015). *Behavior Assessment System for Children—Third Edition (BASC-3): Behavioral and Emotional Screening System (BESS).* Retrieved from http://www.pearsonclinical.com/education/products/100001402/behavior-assessment-system-for-children-third-edition-basc-3.html

Kern, L., & Wehby, J.H. (2014). Using data to intensify behavioral interventions for individual students. *Teaching Exceptional Children, 46*(4), 45–53. doi: 10.1177/0040059914522970

Kettler, R.J., Elliott, S.N., & Albers, C. (2008). Structured teacher ratings to identify students who need help: Validation of the Brief Academic Competence Evaluation Screening System. *Journal of Psychoeducational Assessment, 26*(3), 260–273.

Knoff, H.M. (1990). *The Stop & Think Social Skills Program.* Little Rock, AR: Project ACHIEVE Press.

Knoster, T. (2014). *The teacher's pocket guide for effective classroom management* (2nd ed.). Baltimore, MD: Paul H. Brooks Publishing Co.

Koegel, L.K., Koegel, R.L., & Dunlap, G. (1996). *Positive behavioral support: Including people with difficult behavior in the community.* Baltimore, MD: Paul H Brookes Publishing Co.

Lane, K.L., Kalberg, J.R., & Menzies, H.M. (2009). *Developing schoolwide programs to prevent and manage problem behaviors: A step-by-step approach.* New York, NY: Guilford Press.

Lane, K.L., Little, M.A., Casey, A.M., Lambert, W., Wehby, J., Weisenbach, J.L., & Phillips, A. (2009). A comparison of systematic screening tools for emotional and behavioral disorders. *Journal of Emotional and Behavioral Disorders, 17,* 93–105.

Lane, K.L., Menzies, H.M., Ennis, R.P., & Bezdek, J. (2013). School-wide systems to promote positive behaviors and facilitate inclusion. *Journal of Curriculum and Instruction, 7*(1), 6–31. doi: 10.3776/joci.2013.v7n1p6-31

May, S., Ard, W., Todd, A.W., Horner, R.H., Glasgow, A., Sugai, G., & Sprague, J.R. (2000). *School-wide information system (SWIS).* Eugene, OR: University of Oregon, Educational and Community Supports.

McDougal, J.L., Bardos, A.N., & Meier, S.T. (2011). *Introduction to BIMAS: Behavior Intervention Monitoring Assessment System.* Toronto, Canada: Multi-Health Systems.

McIntosh, K., Borgmeier, C., Anderson, C.M., Horner, R.H., Rodriguez, B.J., & Tobin, T.J. (2008). Technical adequacy of the functional assessment checklist: Teachers and staff (FACTS) FBA interview measure. *Journal of Positive Behavior Interventions, 10*(1), 33–45.

McIntosh, K., Campbell, A.L., Carter, D.R., & Zumbo, B.D. (2009). Concurrent validity of office discipline referrals and cut points used in school-wide positive behavior support. *Behavioral Disorders, 34*(2), 100–113.

McGinnis, E. (2011a). *Skillstreaming the adolescent: A guide for teaching prosocial skills* (3rd ed.). Champaign, IL: Research Press.

McGinnis, E. (2011b). *Skillstreaming in early childhood: A guide for teaching prosocial skills* (3rd ed.). Champaign, IL: Research Press.

McGinnis, E. (2011c). *Skillstreaming the elementary school child: A guide for teaching prosocial skills* (3rd ed.). Champaign, IL: Research Press.

Mitchell, B.S., Stormont, M., & Gage, N.A. (2011). Tier two interventions implemented within the context of tiered prevention framework. *Behavioral Disorders, 36*(4), 241–261.

Myles, B.S., Trautman, M.L., & Schelvan, R.L. (2011). *The hidden curriculum: Practical solutions for understanding unstated rules in social situations.* Shawnee Mission, KS: Autism Asperger Publishing Company.

NCS Pearson. (n.d.). *AIMSweb home page*. Retrieved from http://www.aimsweb.com

Oakes, W.P., Lane, K.L., Cox, M., Magrane, A., Jenkins, A., & Hakins, K. (2012). Tier 2 supports to improve motivation and performance of elementary students with behavioral challenges and poor work completion. *Education and Treatment of Children, 35*(4), 547–584.

O'Neill, R.E., Albin, R.W., Storey, K., Horner, R.H., & Sprague, J.R. (2014). *Functional assessment and program development for problem behavior: A practical handbook* (3rd ed.). Stamford, CT: Cengage Learning.

Patel, P.K., & Runge, T.J. (2011, October). *Universal screening for behavior, social, and emotional functioning in a SWPBIS model.* Poster presentation at the annual meeting of the Association of School Psychologists of Pennsylvania, State College.

Riley-Tillman, T.C., Chafouleas, S.M., Sassu, K.A., Chanese, J.A.M., & Glazer, A.D. (2008). Examining the agreement of Direct Behavior Ratings and Systematic Direct Observation data for on-task and disruptive behavior. *Journal of Positive Behavior Interventions, 10,* 136–143. doi: 10.1177/1098300707312542

Shapiro, J.P., Burgoon, J.D., Welker, C.J., & Clough, J.B. (2002). Evaluation of the Peacemakers Program: School-based violence prevention for students in grades four through eight. *Psychology in the Schools, 39,* 87–100.

Simonsen, B., MacSuga-Gage, A.S., Briere III, D.E., Freeman, J., Myers, D., Scott, T.M., & Sugai, G. (2014). Multitiered support framework for teachers' classroom-management practices: Overview and case study of building the triangle for teachers. *Journal of Positive Behavior Interventions, 16,* 179–190.

Simonsen, B., & Meyers, D. (2015). *Classwide positive behavior interventions and supports.* New York, NY: The Guilford Press.

Sinclair, M., Christenson, S., Evelo, D., & Hurley, C. (1998). Dropout prevention for youth with disabilities: Efficacy of a sustained school engagement procedure. *Exceptional Children, 65,* 7–21.

Sure, M.B. (2001). *I Can Problem Solve: An interpersonal cognitive problem solving program* (3rd ed.). Champaign, IL: Research Press.

Umbreit, J., Ferro, J., Liaupsin, C., & Lane, K. (2007). *Functional behavioral assessment and function-based intervention: An effective, practical approach.* Upper Saddle River, NJ: Prentice Hall.

Walker, H.M., & Holmes, D. (1987). *The Access Program: Adolescent curriculum for communication and effective social skills.* Austin, TX: PRO-ED Publishing.

Walker, H.M., & Severson, H. (1992). *Systematic Screening for Behavior Disorders: User's guide and technical manual.* Longmont, CO: Sopris West.

Walker, H.M., Severson, H.H., Feil, E.G., Stiller, B., & Golly, A. (1998). First step to success: Intervening at the point of school entry to prevent antisocial behavior patterns. *Psychology in the Schools, 35*(3), 259–269.

Wehby, J.H., & Kern, L. (2014). Intensive behavior intervention: What is it, what is its evidence base, and why do we need to implement now? *Council for Exceptional Children, 46*(4), 38–44. doi: 10.1177/0040059914523956

Winner, M.G. (2006). *Think Social!* Mt. Laurel, NJ: Think Social Publishing.

Appendix

Blank Forms

Behavior Progress Report (Primary Classroom)

Name: _____

Date: _____

☺ = 2 points
☺ = 1 point
☹ = 0 points

Points Received: _____

Points Reached: _____

Daily Goal Reached?   YES   NO

Be responsible:	Early morning			Late morning			Early afternoon			Late afternoon			Daily total
Keep my hands, feet, body, and objects to myself.	☺	☺	☹	☺	☺	☹	☺	☺	☹	☺	☺	☹	☺ = ___ ☺ = ___ ☹ = ___
Say nice things to other people.	☺	☺	☹	☺	☺	☹	☺	☺	☹	☺	☺	☹	☺ = ___ ☺ = ___ ☹ = ___
Follow adult directions the first time.	☺	☺	☹	☺	☺	☹	☺	☺	☹	☺	☺	☹	☺ = ___ ☺ = ___ ☹ = ___
							Grand total						☺ = ___ ☺ = ___ ☹ = ___

From Knoster, T. (2014). *The teacher's pocket guide for effective classroom management* (2nd ed., p. 124). Baltimore, MD: Paul H. Brookes Publishing Co., Inc.; reprinted by permission.

In *The Teacher's Pocket Guide for Positive Behavior Support: Targeted Classroom Solutions*, by Tim Knoster & Robin Drogan. (2016; Paul H. Brookes Publishing Co., Inc.)

Behavior Progress Report (Intermediate/Middle Level Classroom)

Student name: _____

Teacher name: _____

2 = Excellent
1 = Satisfactory
0 = Unsatisfactory

Expectation	Date			Date			Date			Date			Date			Weekly total
Keep hands, feet, body, and objects to self.	2	1	0	2	1	0	2	1	0	2	1	0	2	1	0	2 = ___ 1 = ___ 0 = ___
Say nice things to others.	2	1	0	2	1	0	2	1	0	2	1	0	2	1	0	2 = ___ 1 = ___ 0 = ___
Follow adult directions the first time.	2	1	0	2	1	0	2	1	0	2	1	0	2	1	0	2 = ___ 1 = ___ 0 = ___
								Grand weekly total								2 = ___ 1 = ___ 0 = ___

From Knoster, T. (2014). *The teacher's pocket guide for effective classroom management* (2nd ed., p. 125). Baltimore, MD: Paul H. Brookes Publishing Co., Inc.; adapted by permission.

In *The Teacher's Pocket Guide for Positive Behavior Support: Targeted Classroom Solutions*, by Tim Knoster & Robin Drogan. (2016; Paul H. Brookes Publishing Co., Inc.)

Behavior Progress Report
(Multiple Secondary Classrooms)

Student name: _____

Date: _____

2 = Excellent
1 = Satisfactory
0 = Unsatisfactory

Daily Schedule	Keep hands, feet, body, and objects to self.			Say nice things to others.			Follow adult directions the first time.			Class/period total
Homeroom	2	1	0	2	1	0	2	1	0	_____/6
Period 1	2	1	0	2	1	0	2	1	0	_____/6
Period 2	2	1	0	2	1	0	2	1	0	_____/6
Period 3	2	1	0	2	1	0	2	1	0	_____/6
Period 4	2	1	0	2	1	0	2	1	0	_____/6
Lunch	2	1	0	2	1	0	2	1	0	_____/6
Period 5	2	1	0	2	1	0	2	1	0	_____/6
Period 6	2	1	0	2	1	0	2	1	0	_____/6
Period 7	2	1	0	2	1	0	2	1	0	_____/6
Period 8	2	1	0	2	1	0	2	1	0	_____/6
Daily totals	_____/20			_____/20			_____/20			
						Grand daily total				_____/60

From Knoster, T. (2014). *The teacher's pocket guide for effective classroom management* (2nd ed., p. 125). Baltimore, MD: Paul H. Brookes Publishing Co., Inc.; adapted by permission.

In *The Teacher's Pocket Guide for Positive Behavior Support: Targeted Classroom Solutions,* by Tim Knoster & Robin Drogan. (2016; Paul H. Brookes Publishing Co., Inc.)

Resources

POSITIVE BEHAVIOR SUPPORT AND POSITIVE BEHAVIOR INTERVENTIONS AND SUPPORTS

Publications

Bambara, L.M., Janney, R., & Snell, M.E. (2015). *Teachers' guides to inclusive practices: Behavior support* (3rd ed.). Baltimore, MD: Paul H. Brookes Publishing Co.

Bambara, L., & Kern, L. (Eds.). (2005). *Individualized supports for students with problem behaviors: Designing positive behavior plans.* New York, NY: Guilford Press.

Bradshaw, C.P., Koth, C.W., Bevans, K.B., Ialongo, N., & Leaf, P.J. (2008). The impact of school-wide positive behavioral interventions and supports (PBIS) on the organizational health of elementary schools. *School Psychology Quarterly, 23,* 462–473.

Bradshaw, C.P., Mitchell, M.M., & Leaf, P.J. (2010). Examining the effects of school-wide positive behavioral interventions and supports on student outcomes results from a randomized controlled effectiveness trial in elementary schools. *Journal of Positive Behavior Interventions, 3,* 133–148.

Carr, E.G., Dunlap, G., Horner, R.H., Koegel, R.L., Turnbull, A.P., Sailor, W.,…& Fox, L. (2002). Positive behavior support: Evolution of an applied science. *Journal of Positive Behavior Interventions, 4,* 4–16.

Conroy, M.A., Sutherland, K.S., Snyder, A.L., & Marsh, S. (2008). Classwide interventions: Effective instruction makes a difference. *Teaching Exceptional Children, 40,* 24–30.

Crone, D.A., Hawken, L.S., & Horner, R.H. (2010). *Responding to problem behavior in schools: The Behavior Education Program.* New York, NY: Guilford Press.

Knoster, T.P. (2014). *The teacher's pocket guide for effective classroom management* (2nd ed.). Baltimore, MD: Paul H. Brookes Publishing Co.

Sailor, W., Dunlap, G., Sugai, G., & Horner, R. (Eds.). (2009). *Handbook of positive behavior support.* New York, NY: Springer Science and Business Media.

Thurlow, M.L., Christenson, S.L., Sinclair, M.F., & Evelo, D.L. (1997). Wanting the unwanted: Keeping those "out of here" kids in school. *Beyond Behavior, 8*(3), 10–16.

Waasdorp, T.E., Bradshaw, C.P., & Leaf, P.J. (2012). The impact of school-wide positive behavioral interventions and supports on bullying and peer rejection: A randomized controlled effectiveness trial. *Archive of Pediatric Adolescent Medicine, 166*(2), 149–156.

Web Sites

Association for Positive Behavior Support:
http://www.apbs.org

National Association of School Psychologists:
http://www.nasponline.org

Positive Behavioral Interventions and Support OSEP Technical Assistance Center:
http://www.pbis.org

STRATEGIES FOR TIER 2 SUPPORT

Publications

Bruhm, A.L., Lane, K.L., & Hirsh, S.E. (2014). A review of Tier 2 interventions conducted within multitiered models of behavior prevention. *Journal of Emotional and Behavioral Disorders, 22*, 171–189.

Carr, E.G., Levin, L., McConnachie, G., Calson, J.I., Kemp, D.C., & Smith, C.E. (1994). *Communication-based intervention for problem behavior: A user's guide for producing positive change.* Baltimore, MD: Paul H. Brookes Publishing Co.

Chafouleas, S., & Riley-Tillman, C. (2010). *Direct Behavior Rating.* Retrieved from http://www.directbehaviorratings.com

Chafouleas, S., Riley-Tillman, C., Sassu, K., LaFrance, M., & Patwa, S. (2007). Daily behavior report cards: An investigation of the consistency of on-task data across raters and methods. *Journal of Positive Behavior Interventions, 9*, 30–37.

Christenson, S., & Carroll, E.B. (1999). Strengthening the family-school partnership through Check and Connect. In E. Frydenberg (Ed.), *Learning to cope: Developing as a person in complex societies* (pp. 248–273). London, UK: Oxford University Press.

Filter, K.J., McKenna, M.K., Benedict, E.A., Horner, R.H., Todd, A.W., & Watson, J. (2007). Check In/Check Out: A post-hoc evaluation of an efficient, secondary-level targeted intervention for reducing problem behaviors in schools. *Education and Treatment of Children, 30*, 69–84.

Hawken, L.S., MacLeod, K.S., & Rawlings, L. (2007). Effects of the Behavior Education Program (BEP) on problem behavior with elementary school students. *Journal of Positive Behavior Interventions, 9*, 94–101.

Lane, K.L., Cook, B.G., & Tankersley, M. (Eds.). (2013). *Research-based strategies for improving outcomes in behavior.* New York, NY: Pearson.

Lehr, C.A., Sinclair, M.F., & Christenson, S.L. (2004). Addressing student engagement and truancy prevention during the elementary years: A replication study of the Check & Connect model. *Journal of Education for Students Placed At Risk, 9*(3), 279–301.

Lyst, A.M., Gabriel, S., O'Shaughnessy, T.E., Meyers, J., & Meyers, B. (2005). Social validity: Perceptions of Check and Connect with early literacy support. *Journal of School Psychology, 43*(3), 197–218.

McCurdy, B.L., Kunsch, C., & Reibstein, S. (2007). Secondary prevention in the urban school: Implementing the Behavior Education Program. *Preventing School Failure, 51,* 12–19.

McIntosh, K., Campbell, A., Carter, D., & Dickey, C. (2009). Differential effects of a Tier 2 behavioral intervention based on function of problem behavior. *Journal of Positive Behavior Interventions, 11,* 82–93.

O'Neill, R.E., Horner, R.H., Albin, R.W., Sprague, J.R., & Newton, J.S. (1997). *Functional assessment and program development for problem behavior: A practical handbook.* Pacific Grove, CA: Brooks/Cole.

Todd, A.W., Campbell, A.L., Meyer, G., & Horner, R.H. (2008). The effects of a targeted intervention to reduce problem behaviors: Elementary school implementation of Check-In/Check Out. *Journal of Positive Behavioral Interventions, 10,* 46–55.

Web Sites

National Center on Intensive Intervention at American Institutes for Research:
http://www.intensiveintervention.org

PBISApps—The Makers of the SWIS Suite:
http://www.pbisapps.org

INDIVIDUALIZED INTENSIVE (TIER 3) SUPPORTS

Bambara, L.M., Janney, R., & Snell, M. (2015). *Teachers' guides to inclusive practices: Behavior support* (3rd ed.). Baltimore, MD: Paul H. Brookes Publishing Co.

Bambara, L.M., & Knoster, T. (2009). *Designing positive behavior support plans.* Washington, DC: American Association on Intellectual and Developmental Disabilities.

Dunlap, G., Iovannone, R., Kincaid, D., Wilson, K., Christiansen, K., Strain, P., & English, C. (2010). *Prevent-Teach-Reinforce: The school-based model of individualized positive behavior support.* Baltimore, MD: Paul H. Brookes Publishing Co.

Scott, T.M., Liaupsin, C., & Nelson, C.M. (2001). *Behavior intervention planning: Using the outcomes of functional behavior assessment.* Longmont, CO: Sopris West Educational Services.

ACADEMIC AND BEHAVIORAL SCREENING AND PROGRESS MONITORING

Publications

Kamphaus, R.W., & Reynolds, C.R. (2015). *Behavior Assessment System for Children—Third Edition (BASC-3): Behavioral and Emotional Screening System (BESS).* Bloomington, MN: Pearson.

Kettler, R.J., Elliott, S.N., & Albers, C. (2008). Structured teacher ratings to identify students who need help: Validation of the Brief Academic Competence Evaluation Screening System. *Journal of Psychoeducational Assessment, 26*(3), 260–273.

McDougal, J.L., Bardos, A.N., & Meier, S.T. (2011). *Introduction to BIMAS: Behavior Intervention Monitoring Assessment System.* Toronto, Canada: Multi-Health Systems.

Web Sites

AIMSweb:
http://www.aimsweb.com

Behavior Assessment System for Children—Third Edition (BASC-3):
http://www.pearsonclinical.com/education/products/100001402/
behavior-assessment-system-for-children-third-edition-basc-3.html

Behavior Intervention Monitoring Assessment System (BIMAS):
http://www.mhs.com/product.aspx?gr=edu&prod=bimas&id=overview

Behavioral and Emotional Rating Scale–Second Edition (BERS-2):
http://www.proedinc.com/customer/productView.aspx?ID=3430

Dynamic Indicators of Basic Early Literacy Skills (DIBELS):
http://www.dibels.org

Social Skills Improvement System (SSIS):
http://www.pearsonclinical.com/education/products/100000322/
social-skills-improvement-system-ssis-rating-scales.html

Strengths and Difficulties Questionnaire (SDQ):
http://www.sdqinfo.com

Student Risk Screening Scale (SRSS):
http://miblsi.cenmi.org/MiBLSiModel/Evaluation/Measures
/StudentRiskScreeningScale.aspx

Systematic Screening for Behavior Disorders (SSBD):
http://www.nhcebis.seresc.net/universal_ssbd

RESOURCES FOR CURRICULUM-BASED MEASUREMENT AND CURRICULUM-BASED ASSESSMENT

Publications

Ardoin, S.P., Christ, T.J., Morena, L.S., Cormier, D.C., & Klingbeil, D.A. (2013). A systematic review and summarization of the recommendations and research surrounding curriculum-based measurement of oral reading fluency (CBM-R) decision rule. *Journal of School Psychology, 51*(1), 1–18.

Christ, T.J., Zopluoglu, C., Long, J.D., & Monaghen, B.D. (2012). Curriculum-based measurement of oral reading: Quality of progress monitoring outcomes. *Exceptional Children, 78*(3), 356–373.

Hargis, C.H. (2013). *Curriculum-based assessment: A primer.* Springfield, IL: Charles C. Thomas.

Shaprio, E.S. (2011). *Academic skills problems: Direct assessment and intervention.* New York, NY: Guilford Press.

Web Sites

Intervention Central:
http://www.interventioncentral.org/curriculum-based-measurement
-reading-math-assesment-tests

The National Center on Student Progress Monitoring:
http://www.studentprogress.org

RTI Action Network:
http://www.rtinetwork.org/essential/assessment/progress

Index

Page numbers followed by *f* and *t* indicate figures and tables, respectively.